# MAHATMA GANDHI
## Indian Leader and World Influence

Mahatma Gandhi, the leader of India's hard-won
struggle for independence, died at the hand of an
assassin on January 30, 1948. But the inspiration of
his life and his spiritual teachings live on in the
hearts of millions throughout the world.

This moving biography of Gandhi, by a man who
knew him well, is written with warmth and simplicity. It tells the whole story of this great man from
his boyhood days in India before he went to London
to study law, through his experiences in South Africa where he worked to achieve legal equality for
Indians and Negroes with white men, to the exciting years in India when he put his extraordinary
gifts to use in the cause of India's independence.

In telling of Gandhi's later years the author makes
clear the problems of a complex country at a crucial
period of its history and dramatically reveals the
deep spirituality, the high and devoted purpose,
and the extraordinary humanity of one of the most
remarkable men of modern times. And he shows the
real significance of Gandhi's teachings for each of
us—his emphasis on kindness, honesty, humility,
non-violence, and the exaltation of the individual
human spirit.

**LOUIS FISCHER** who first visited Gandhi in 1942
and again in 1946, was an outstanding foreign correspondent and analyst of world affairs, and the author of a number of books.

# INDIA and PAKISTAN

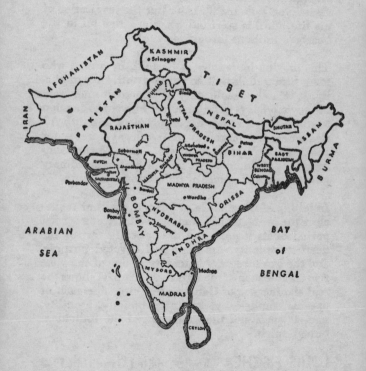

# GANDHI

*His Life and Message for the World*

### By LOUIS FISCHER
*Author of The Life of Mahatma Gandhi*

A MENTOR BOOK

**NEW AMERICAN LIBRARY**

NEW YORK AND SCARBOROUGH, ONTARIO

SIGNET, SIGNET CLASSIC, MENTOR, ONYX, PLUME, MERIDIAN AND
NAL BOOKS are published *in the United States* by
NAL PENGUIN INC.,
1633 Broadway, New York, New York 10019,
*in Canada* by The New American Library of Canada Limited,
81 Mack Avenue, Scarborough, Ontario M1L 1M8

FIRST MENTOR PRINTING, JANUARY, 1954

33  34  35  36  37  38  39  40  41

PRINTED IN THE UNITED STATES OF AMERICA

# CONTENTS

# PART ONE
# From Birth to Greatness

## 1 The World Weeps

By the holy waters of the Jumna, near New Delhi, almost a million people waited in the sun for the funeral procession to reach the cremation grounds. White predominated —the white of women's cotton saris and of men's clothes, caps, and bulbous turbans.

At Rajghat, a few hundred feet from the river, a fresh pyre had been built of stone, brick, and earth. It was eight feet square and about two feet high. Long, thin sandalwood logs sprinkled with incense were stacked on it. Mahatma Gandhi's body lay on the pyre with his head to the north. In that position Buddha met his end.

At 4:45 P.M., Ramdas, the third son of the Mahatma, set fire to the funeral pyre. The logs burst into flames. The vast assemblage groaned. Women wailed; men wept. The wood crackled and seethed and the flames united into a single fire.

Now there was silence. Gandhi's body was being reduced to ashes and cinders.

A day earlier, on January 30, 1948, a young man had shot and killed Mohandas K. Gandhi, India's leader.

"I never saw Gandhi," wrote Léon Blum, a former French Premier. "I do not know his language. I never set foot in his country, and yet I feel the same sorrow as if I had lost someone near and dear. The whole world has been plunged into mourning by the death of this extraordinary man."

When he died, Gandhi was what he had always been: a private citizen without wealth, property, title, official position, academic distinction, or scientific achievement. Yet the chiefs of all governments, except of the Soviet government, and the heads of all religions paid homage to the thin

brown man of seventy-eight in a loincloth. President
Truman, the British King, the President of France, the
Archbishop of Canterbury, Pope Pius, the Chief Rabbi of
London, the Dalai Lama of Tibet, and more than three
thousand other foreigners sent unsolicited messages of
condolence to India. The Security Council of the United
Nations interrupted its deliberations to pay tribute to
Gandhi. Philip Noel-Baker, the British delegate, lauded
Gandhi as "the friend of the poorest, the loneliest, and the
lost." Gandhi's "greatest achievements," he declared, "are
still to come." Other representatives in the Security Council
praised his devotion to peace and his spiritual qualities.

The U.N. lowered its flag to half-mast.

Humanity lowered its flag.

The mourners were aware of some of the Mahatma's
attributes. Gandhi "made humility and truth more powerful
than empires," said U.S. Senator Arthur H. Vandenberg.
"I know no other man of any time or indeed in recent history," Sir Stafford Cripps, British statesman, declared,
"who so forcefully and convincingly demonstrated the
power of spirit over material things." General George C.
Marshall, then U.S. Secretary of State, groping to explain
the world's bereavement, said, "Mahatma Gandhi was the
spokesman for the conscience of mankind."

Men and women and children knew, or felt, that when
Gandhi fell by the assassin's three bullets the conscience of
mankind had been left without a spokesman. Humanity
was impoverished because a poor man had died. No one
who survived him had faced mighty adversaries at home
and abroad with the weapons of kindness, honesty, humility, and nonviolence, and, with these alone, won so many
victories. His is a story of unusual success with unusual
means.

## 2   Blundering Boy

If Gandhi had lived in India three thousand years ago his
birth would have been wrapped in myths and his youth in
miracles. But the cold light of the nineteenth century shows
that his origin was ordinary, his childhood normal, his
student days uneventful, and his early professional career

a failure. "The child is father of the man," and Mohandas the schoolboy and teen-ager obviously sired the Mahatma, yet nobody could have predicted that he would. He seemed to have little ability and less talent.

Mohandas Karamchand Gandhi was born on October 2, 1869, in Porbandar, a small, seaside town in the Kathiawar Peninsula in western India, about halfway between Bombay and Karachi. Kathiawar lay off the beaten track, remote from European influence; it was still divided into a large number of city-states ruled by native princelings who behaved like petty autocrats to their subjects and quaking sycophants before the British. Porbandar (population 72,077, according to the 1872 census) was one such minuscule domain; Rajkot (population 36,770) another, and Wankaner (28,750) a third. At different times in his career, Karamchand Gandhi, father of the Mahatma, served as prime minister to the raja or rana of these little realms.

Mohandas wrote in later years that his father "had no education save that of experience" and was even "innocent" of history and geography, but remained "incorruptible and had earned a reputation for strict impartiality in his family as well as outside." Moreover, the son added, "he was a lover of his clan, truthful, brave and generous, but short-tempered."

Karamchand, the politician, married Putlibai, a devout, illiterate, Hindu girl. Mohandas, their fourth and last child, always remembered his mother's "saintliness" and her "deeply religious" nature. Putlibai attended temple services every day and never ate without prayer. Long fasts did not dismay her. During the annual Chaturmas, a kind of Lent lasting through the four-month rainy season, she habitually took only a single meal a day, and one year, in addition, she observed a fast on alternate days.

The family was well-to-do. Karamchand owned a home in Porbandar, another in Rajkot, and another in Kutiana. Karamchand wore a gold necklace, and a brother of Mohandas had a heavy, solid-gold armlet. Mohandas had his own nurse and his own concertina.

At school in Porbandar, Gandhi found it difficult to learn the multiplication table. "My intellect must have been sluggish, and my memory raw," the Mahatma wrote about himself as a primary-grade pupil. A year later when the family moved to Rajkot, he was a "mediocre student" but very punctual.

The boy Mohandas was shy. "My books and lessons were my sole companions," he recalled as an adult. At the end of the school day, he ran home. He lacked the confidence and poise to talk to anybody; "I was even afraid lest anyone poke fun at me."

As he grew older, however, he found friends and played in the streets and by the sea. He spun tops and played with rubber balloons. He was quiet and obedient; "I had learned to carry out the orders of elders, not to scan their actions." Nevertheless, he began to smoke secretly at the age of twelve and stole money from his parents and elder brothers to buy cigarettes.

Once he and a young relative learned that the seeds of a jungle plant named dhatura were poisonous. So they joined in a suicide pact which would rid them forever of parental domination. Moved by a sense of the dramatic, they decided to die in the temple. They actually went to the shrine with the mortal seeds in their pockets. But at the last moment courage failed them. For self-respect, each swallowed two or three seeds and walked home.

Presently, serious matters claimed the child's attention. Mohandas Karamchand Gandhi married at the age of thirteen when he was a high school sophomore. The bride, Kasturbai, was thirteen too. Their parents made the match but did not tell them about it until the wedding preparations were complete. "My brother's wife had thoroughly coached me about my behavior," Gandhi wrote forty years after the event. "I do not know who had coached my wife." Both were nervous, and "the coaching could not carry me far," he added. "But no coaching is really necessary in such matters. The impressions of the former birth are potent enough to make all coaching superfluous."

"Two innocent children all unwittingly hurled themselves on the ocean of life," with only, presumably, their experiences in a former incarnation to guide them. Thus Gandhi described "the cruel custom of child marriage." It was made possible by the Indian institution of the joint family under which parents and their children and their sons' wives and children, sometimes numbering thirty or more persons, lived within the same house. Adolescent newlyweds like

Mohandas and Kasturbai therefore did not have to worry about an apartment, furniture, or board. (Subsequently, the British government raised the minimum age of marriage.)

"I lost no time in assuming the authority of a husband," the grown Mr. Gandhi reminisced. Kasturbai "could not go out without my permission." So when the thirteen-year-old Kasturbai wished to play games in the street she had to ask her thirteen-year-old husband, and he would frequently say no, for he was jealous. But she was headstrong and "made it a point to go out whenever and wherever she liked." He, consequently, got "more and more cross"; sometimes they did not speak to one another for days.

In those years, Gandhi later admitted, "I used to be haunted by fear of thieves, ghosts, and serpents. I did not dare to stir out of doors at night." His young wife had no such fears. "I felt ashamed of myself," he wrote. He was short and thin, and disliked cricket and gymnastics, which were compulsory in high school. But he had read that walking in the open air was good for the health, and he formed the habit. "These walks gave me a fairly hardy constitution."

Still he envied the strong, big boys, and especially a Moslem friend, Sheik Mehtab, who excelled in distance running and in the broad and high jump. These exploits dazzled Gandhi as did Sheik's boast that he could hold live snakes in his hands and feared neither burglar nor ghost. What accounted for such bravery? He ate meat. Gandhi's religion forbade him to eat meat. He had never touched it.

Though British rule operated indirectly and almost invisibly in Kathiawar, Gandhi's schoolmates had already learned to respect and oppose the British. They recited a poem which went:

> Behold the mighty Englishman,
> He rules the Indian small,
> Because being a meat-eater
> He is five cubits tall.

Either because he wanted to expel the British or reinforce his own physique and courage, Gandhi finally succumbed to Sheik Mehtab's temptations and went with him to a secluded spot on the river where Mohandas chewed and chewed the cooked goat's flesh which Sheik had brought

and ultimately swallowed it. He became sick immediately.
That night he had a recurrent dream of a live goat bleating
in his stomach. Nevertheless he considered that "meat-
eating was a duty" and performed it for a year at secret
rendezvous with Sheik. Then the dissimulation and dis-
honesty repelled him and he abandoned meat consumption
until he could resume it openly after his parents' death.

Meat-eating was part of Gandhi's revolt against religion.
He disliked the "glitter and pomp" of Hindu temples and
confessed that he had no "living faith in God." Who made
the world? he asked. Who directed it? Nobody gave him a
satisfactory answer, nor did the sacred books he consulted.
He accordingly inclined "somewhat toward atheism." Keeping an open mind, however, he listened to his father's frequent argumentations with Moslem, Parsi, and Jain friends
who came to the house to discuss the differences between
their faiths and Hinduism. Jainism, a Hindu reform church,
prohibits the killing of any living creature. Jain priests wear
white gauze masks over their mouths so as not to breathe
in, and thus kill, an insect, and they are not supposed to
walk out in the dark lest they unintentionally step on a
worm. Jain influence was strong in Kathiawar, and Gandhi,
always a great absorber, imbibed some Jain as well as
Buddhist ideas during his short rebellion against Hinduism.

Gandhi's father Karamchand died in 1885 after an illness
lasting several years in which the family fortunes declined;
he left little property. Now the question of Mohandas' professional education arose. Gandhi showed an interest in
medicine. But his brother recalled their father's objection
to the dissection of dead bodies. Would it not be better to
study law? Gandhi's grandfather Uttamchand had been
prime minister of Porbandar and handed the office down to
his son Karamchand, who passed it to his brother Tulsidas.
The job was almost family property, and if Mohandas became an attorney he would be practically assured of the
prime ministership of his home state. But, being insecure,
he was afraid of the law. Could he pass the examinations?
At this juncture a friend of the family suggested that a
quick, three-year course in England held the best promise
of professional and political success. The prospect of a stay
abroad thrilled Gandhi. An uncle, who was now the head
of the family, objected that European-trained lawyers

dressed "as shamelessly as Englishmen," forsook Indian traditions, and never appeared without a cigar in their mouth. Still, if Putlibai agreed, he would sanction the trip. She entertained doubts about young men's morals in England. Here a Jain monk named Becharji Swami came to the rescue by administering an oath to Gandhi that he would not touch wine, women, or meat.

There was some difficulty about funds until Laxmidas, Mohandas' elder brother and a lawyer, undertook to supply them. Together they traveled to Bombay where Gandhi would board ship for England. New troubles developed. The Gandhis were members of the Modh Bania subcaste and when the Modh Banias of Bombay heard of Mohandas' projected trip abroad they protested. No Modh Bania had ever been to England, the elders contended, because Hinduism could not be practiced there. But Gandhi, defiant, told them at one of their meetings that he would go. The headman thereupon ostracized him by saying, "This boy shall be treated as an outcaste from today."

Undaunted, Gandhi bought a steamer ticket, a short British jacket, a necktie, and enough food, chiefly fruit and sweets, for the three weeks to Southampton. He sailed on September 4, 1888, a month before his nineteenth birthday. A few months earlier, Kasturbai had borne him a male child, and they called it Harilal.

## 3   Gandhi in London

Gandhi was photographed in London shortly after arriving there. His hair is black, thick, and carefully parted a little to the right of center. The ears are big. The nose is big and pointed. The lips and eyes are impressive. The eyes seem to mirror puzzlement, fright, yearning; they appear to move in search of something. The lips are full, sensuous, sad, and defensive. He looks like a man without compass or focus. He has been injured or is afraid of injury. The face is that of a person who fears coming struggles within himself and with the world. He wonders whether he can conquer his passions, whether he will make good.

British life was very foreign to the young Gandhi. His

autobiography records his attempt and failure to adjust to
it. He bought a top hat, spats, striped trousers, a morning
coat, a silver-mounted cane, silk shirts, and leather gloves.
He spent ten pounds for an evening suit made to order in
Bond Street and invested three pounds in a course of dancing lessons. But "I could not follow the piano," he confessed, or "achieve anything like rhythmic motion." Hoping
to develop an ear for music, he purchased a violin and
found a teacher. Before long he sold the instrument. A
similar effort to learn elocution ended just as quickly.

Gandhi always craved harmony with his surroundings.
That is why, years later, he adopted the loincloth as his
garb. Tens of millions of Indian peasants wear nothing else.
In London, Gandhi was admittedly "aping the British gentleman," on the assumption that it would raise his status and
bring him into key with what he mistakenly regarded as
the dominant note in British life.

At the same time he was capable of strong resistance to
conformity. English acquaintances urged him to eat meat,
but he refused to break the vow he had given his mother.
In fact, he became a zealous vegetarian and, after some
wavering, rejected even eggs and dishes—cakes and pud-
dings—made with eggs, because they came under the meat
ban: eggs were potential living creatures. This additional
privation and the consequent monotony of diet were canceled by the "inner relish, distinctly more healthy, delicate,
and permanent" than food, which he got from observing
the vow.

He learned to cook; carrot soup was a specialty. Sweets
and spices had been arriving by sea from his family in
India. He asked that the sendings be discontinued and
began instead to eat and enjoy spinach and other vegetables
without condiments. "Many such experiments," he remarked, "taught me that the real seat of taste was not in
the tongue but in the mind," and Gandhi had commenced
that remarkable lifelong task of changing his mind.

Other transformations were taking place. He had already
traversed "the Sahara of atheism" and emerged thirsting for
religion. He met Madam H. P. Blavatsky and Mrs. Annie
Besant and read their books on theosophy but was not
converted; he preferred Hinduism. A British Bible sales-
man persuaded him to read the Old and New Testaments.

Leviticus and Numbers bored him and he got no further (until, as a mahatma, he reveled in the Prophets, Psalms, and Ecclesiastes). He found the New Testament more interesting, and the Sermon on the Mount "went straight to my heart." ". . . resist not evil, but whosoever shall smite thee on thy right cheek, turn to him the left also. . . . Blessed are the meek. . . . Blessed are ye when men shall revile you and persecute you. . . . Agree with thine adversary quickly. . . . Forgive men their trespasses. . . . Lay not up for yourself treasure upon earth . . . for where your treasure is, there will your heart be also. . . ." These words of Christ "delighted" the mahatma-to-be. They reminded him of the *Bhagavad-Gita,* the sacred book of the Hindus, which, he admitted to his shame, he had not read until his second year as a law student in London. It produced a tremendous impact which remained throughout life. "When doubts haunt me, when disappointments stare me in the face, and I see not one ray of hope on the horizon," he wrote in his weekly magazine, *Young India,* of August 6, 1925, "I turn to the *Bhagavad-Gita,* and find a verse to comfort me; and I immediately begin to smile in the midst of overwhelming sorrow." Mahadev Desai, for many years the Mahatma's secretary, testifies that "every moment of Gandhi's life is a conscious effort to live the message of the *Gita.*" Gandhi called it his "spiritual reference book."

The *Bhagavad-Gita* or Celestial Song is an exquisite poem of seven hundred stanzas about the science and practice of yoga. Written by one person some time, according to scholars, between the fifth and second centuries B.C., the *Gita* is a battlefield conversation between its hero, Krishna, who is worshipped in India as a god, and Arjuna, the chief of a faction in a famous civil war. "Krishna," says Sir Sarvapalli Radhakrishnan, the Hindu philosopher, "is the human embodiment of Vishnu," the Supreme God.

The tale of Krishna's life on earth mingles legend with hazy prehistoric fact. God, the story says, incarnated himself in the womb of an Indian king's sister, and Krishna was thus born without the intervention of man. But the king, fearing a rival, had ordered all newborn royal children done to death, and Krishna was therefore secretly transferred by divine hand to the family of a lowly herdsman in place of its own infant daughter. The child Krishna defeated

all the nether world's efforts to destroy him. Once during a
flood he lifted a mountain with his little finger and held it
up for seven days and nights so that the people might save
themselves and their animals. Not suspecting his divinity,
all the village maidens loved him and danced with him.
Grown to young manhood, Krishna killed his tyrant uncle
and won universal renown. Ultimately he went into retire-
ment in a forest where a hunter, mistaking him for a deer,
shot an arrow into his heel. As the huntsman drew near and
recognized Krishna, he was stricken with grief, but Krishna
smiled, blessed him, and died.

The *Gita* opens with Krishna on the battlefield serving
as Arjuna's unarmed charioteer. Opposite are Arjuna's
royal cousins arrayed for the fratricidal fray. Arjuna is
loath to fight. He says to Krishna:

> I have unhappy forebodings, O Keshava,
> and I see no good in slaying kinsmen in battle.
> I seek not victory, nor sovereign power, nor earthly
>     joys.
> What good are sovereign power, worldly pleasures
>     and
> even life to us, O Govinda?

Keshava and Govinda are among the many names of Lord
Krishna.

Overcome by revulsion against killing his own relatives,
Arjuna announces, "I will not fight."

The Lord Krishna remonstrates with him:

> Thou mournest for them whom thou shouldst not
>     mourn,
> and utterest vain words of wisdom. The wise mourn
>     neither
> for the living nor for the dead.
> For never was I not, nor thou nor these kings, nor
> will any of us cease to be hereafter.

Death, in other words, matters little; the soul, or atman,
Krishna explains, is immortal and unattainable by man's
weapons of destruction. Calling the soul "This," Krishna
says,

> This is never born nor having been will
> ever not be any more; unborn, eternal, everlasting,
> ancient, This is not slain when the body is slain. . . .

As a man casts off worn-out garments and takes
others that
are new, even so the embodied one casts off worn-out
bodies and passes on to others new.

That, succinctly, is the Hindu doctrine of the transmigration
of the soul. Krishna adds:

This no weapons wound; This no fire burns; This no
waters wet, This no wind doth dry. . . .
For certain is the death of the born, and certain is the
birth of the dead; therefore what is unavoidable thou
shouldst not regret.

Besides, Krishna emphasizes, Arjuna is a member of the
Hindu warrior caste, the Kshatriyas, and it is his duty to
fight.

The orthodox Hindu interpretation of the *Gita* as a divine summons to caste obligation and killing was repugnant
to Gandhi and even when he first read the book in London
in 1888-89 he called it an allegory in which the battlefield is
the soul and Arjuna man's higher impulses struggling
against evil. In any case, Arjuna was still puzzled by
Krishna's argument that since corporeal death is not death
he need not hesitate to go to war. What would be gained?
Krishna answers:

For me, O Partha, there is naught to do in the
three worlds, nothing worth gaining that I have
not gained; yet I am ever in action.

The ideal is action in a just cause without thought of advantage. Krishna says,

Hold alike pleasure and pain, gain and loss, victory
and defeat, and gird thy loins for the fight; so
doing thou shalt not incur sin.

That is one aspect of yoga: selflessness in action. Krishna
says,

Act thou, O Dhananjaya [Arjuna] without attachment,
steadfast in Yoga, even-minded in success and failure,
Even-mindedness is Yoga.

Krishna describes the Yogi as one
> Whose mind is untroubled in sorrow and longeth
> not for joys, who is free from passion, fear,
> and wrath—he is called the ascetic of
> secure understanding. The man who sheds all long-
>    ings and moves without
> concern, free from the sense of "I" and "Mine"—
> he attains peace.

There are yogis who meditate and yogis who act. The yogi of action is the karma yogi. Mahatma Gandhi was a karma yogi. In a comment on the *Gita,* Gandhi defined the perfect karma yogi: "He is a devotee who is jealous of none, who is a fount of mercy, who is without egotism, who is selfless, who treats alike cold and heat, happiness and misery, who is ever forgiving, who is always contented, whose resolutions are firm, who has dedicated mind and soul to God, who causes no dread, who is not afraid of others, who is free from exultation, sorrow and fear, who is pure, who is versed in action yet remains unaffected by it, who renounces all fruit, good or bad, who treats friend and foe alike, who is untouched by respect or disrespect, who is not puffed up by praise, who does not go under when people speak ill of him, who loves silence and solitude, who has a disciplined reason. Such devotion is inconsistent with the existence at the same time of strong attachments."

Gandhi summarized it in one word: "Desirelessness."

Desirelessness, or Hindu renunciation, it has been ar-gued, leads to personal indifference and passivity and na-tional poverty and stagnation. Gandhi contended, on the contrary, that to act while renouncing interest in the fruits of action is the best road to success. "He who is ever brood-ing over result," he wrote, "often loses nerve in the perform-ance of duty. He becomes impatient and then gives vent to anger and begins to do unworthy things; he jumps from action to action, never remaining faithful to any. He who broods over results is like a man given to the objects of senses; he is ever-distracted, he says good-by to all scruples, everything is right in his estimation and he therefore re-sorts to means fair and foul to attain his end."

Renunciation, if one is capable of it, creates the inner peace and poise necessary to achieve real lasting results, even material results, untainted by ugly means. For the exceptional practitioner of self-denial a special prize is in store. Krishna declares,

> But there is a unique reward. The great yogis, the
> Mahatmas or Great souls having come to Me,
> reach the highest perfection; they come not
> again to birth, unlasting and abode of misery.

Thus the yogi's highest recompense is to become so firmly united with God after death that he need never again return to the status of migrating mortal man. Several times in his life Gandhi expressed the hope not to be born anew.

Mahatmas are rare. Desirelessness is an ideal to which few in India or anywhere attain or even aspire, but the young Hindu, reciting the *Bhagavad-Gita* several times a month, indeed more frequently perhaps, at home or in the temple, becomes aware of its injunctions and may be inspired, on the threshold of life, to ponder the purpose of life. Gandhi undoubtedly did, and it affected his entire future.

Gandhi's interest in the *Bhagavad-Gita* and his passionate vegetarianism reflect a longing for India. He required identification with surroundings, yet his chief contact in England was with a group of aged, crusading vegetarians who, he later declared, "had the habit of talking of nothing but food and nothing but disease." His studies were a regretted necessity, a ladder to a profession, and they received only a few lines in his reminiscences. He was admitted to the Inner Temple and London University, took courses in French, Latin, physics and chemistry, improved his English, and read Common and Roman Law. Called to the bar on June 10, 1891, he enrolled in the High Court on June 11, and without spending a single extra day in England, sailed for Bombay on June 12.

Life began for Gandhi after college. In his weekly magazine, *Young India,* of September 4, 1924, he wrote that his college days were before the time "when . . . I began life." The two years and eight months in England came at a formative stage and must have left a mark. But their influence was probably less than normal. For Gandhi was not the student type. He was a doer, and he gained knowledge, confidence, and stature through action. Books and people certainly affected him. But the real Gandhi, the Gandhi of history, did not emerge and did not even hint of his existence in the school years. Little, perhaps, was to be expected of the frail provincial Indian transplanted at the green age of nineteen to metropolitan London. Yet the contrast between the mediocre, unimpressive, handicapped, floundering M. K. Gandhi, barrister-at-law, who left England in 1891, and the Mahatma of the twentieth century who led millions is so great as to suggest that until public service tapped his enormous reserves of will power, intuition, energy, self-confidence, and devotion to a cause his true personality lay dormant.

## 4   Two Incidents Shape the Future

When Gandhi returned to India his son Harilal was four. His mother was dead; they had not sent him the sad information because they knew how much he loved her. His wife Kasturbai was a beautiful young woman and he felt more jealous of her than ever. Once they quarreled so fiercely he packed her off from Rajkot to her parents in Porbandar.

As a lawyer he failed both in Rajkot and Bombay. In the latter city he had a ten-dollar case but was literally too shy to open his mouth in court and gave the brief to a colleague. He now began to do odd legal jobs for the ruling prince of Porbandar. Laxmidas, his elder brother, following in the footsteps of their father and grandfather, worked as secretary and adviser to the heir to the throne of Porbandar and seemed to be in line for the prime ministership of his little native realm. But he had antagonized the British Political Agent on whom his fate depended. Mohandas had casually met the agent in London; Laxmidas therefore asked his young brother to visit the agent and intercede for him. Gandhi thought this a wrong thing to do but yielded to his brother's importunings. The agent said if Laxmidas had been wronged he could apply through the proper channels. When Gandhi persisted, the agent told him to leave, and as Gandhi continued to argue, the agent's peon or messenger took hold of him and pushed him out.

The shock of this incident, Gandhi writes in his autobiography, "changed the course of my entire life." For the first time his life had at least negative direction: he knew what he did not want to do. The episode intensified his abhorrence of the petty intrigue, palace pomp, subservience, and snobbery which pervaded the governments of the tiny principalities of Kathiawar. He would not be a fawning sycophant. It poisoned character. He yearned to escape.

Just then a firm of Porbandar Moslems offered to send him to South Africa for a year as their lawyer. He accepted. "I wanted somehow to leave India," he admitted sadly. It was almost two years since he had left London and he was a failure, so he would "try my luck in South Africa," he said.

Shortly after his arrival in South Africa, Gandhi became involved in a second incident ending in defeat and ejection. This time his life acquired positive direction.

A lawsuit required Gandhi's presence in Pretoria, the capital of Transvaal. He boarded the train for the overnight journey and entered a first-class compartment with his first-class ticket. At Maritzburg, in the province of Natal, a white man came into the compartment, looked at the brown intruder, and withdrew to reappear a moment later with two railway officials who ordered Gandhi to go to the baggage car. He protested his first-class ticket but they said he had to leave. He stayed. So they fetched a policeman who threw him and his suitcases onto the station platform.

Many years later, Dr. John R. Mott, an American missionary in India, asked Mahatma Gandhi, "What have been the most creative experiences in your life?" Gandhi told him about the experience at Maritzburg.

Gandhi could have returned to the train and occupied a place in third class. He chose to remain in the station waiting room. The station people had his luggage and overcoat. It was cold in the mountains but he would not ask for his belongings, so he sat through the night shivering and meditating.

These two episodes made the man, yet it is equally true that the man made the episodes. Other Indians had been expelled from a compartment when a white man objected to their presence, and they had accepted lesser accommodations. "You cannot strike your head against a stone wall," his compatriots counseled him the next morning. But when Gandhi encountered injustice at Maritzburg he did not bend, he took avoidable punishment out of which, however,

came a resolution to combat the dread disease of color
prejudice. Intransigence and personal suffering highlighted
the principle at stake and emphasized the need of fighting
for it. Instead of staying a year in South Africa on a law
assignment, he remained from 1893 to 1914, twenty-one
years, during which he not only increased his moral and
intellectual stature many cubits but became a successful
leader and lawyer. In the end he won a great victory for
freedom.

That chilly night in the Maritzburg station waiting room,
the twenty-four-year-old Indian lawyer began to think of
himself as a David assailing the Goliath of racial discrimination. Why Gandhi? What was it that started him up from
Maritzburg to world greatness? Did he want to be morally
strong because he was physically weak? Was he less fet-
tered and more ambitious because his career so far had
borne no fruit? Did he sense untouched talents within and
realize that they would emerge only if harnessed to social
service? Was it luck, destiny, inheritance, the *Bhagavad-
Gita,* or some other immeasurable circumstance? Perhaps
elements of these plus pride, moral indignation, and a feeling of inadequacy combined to make him reach out toward
leadership. The British agent at Porbandar and the white
policeman at Maritzburg were symbols of his and his people's weakness, and he resented it. Whenever Gandhi felt
distressed or disturbed he wanted to do something about it.
In the presence of evil he had to act. Mere headshaking and
handwringing never satisfied him. Passivity riled him. There
was not a single passive fiber in his character, and all his
resistance was active.

## 5  Color Prejudice

Within a week of the Maritzburg incident, Gandhi convened a meeting of the Indians of Pretoria and delivered
an address on white discrimination. It was his first public
speech. Zeal for a cause dissolved his timidity and loosened
his tongue. The audience consisted of Moslem merchants
interspersed with Hindus. His statements bore the mark,
even at that early stage, of the unique qualities of Gandhi's
leadership. He urged them to tell the truth in business,

adopt more sanitary habits, forget religious and caste differences, and learn English. Since his aim was fair treatment for the Indians of South Africa, the Indians, who were the means of achieving that end, first had to improve themselves and discard their own bad habits. Often, in fact, Gandhi was more interested in improving the human means than in attaining political ends. For what does it benefit man if his status is raised when he himself is not raised? Gandhi's ends were actually a means to a better means, a better man. He always tried to exalt the individual; hence "it has always been a mystery to me," he wrote in his autobiography, "how men can feel themselves honored by the humiliation of their fellow-beings." He must have known the answer: some men loom large by lifting up others and some by kicking and humiliating others. It is the difference between the benefactor and the bully, between the mahatma and the dictator.

Persecution, whether by minorities or majorities, results from intolerance of differences and from fears based on lack of self-faith. In a competitive world, most men dislike rivals, nonconformists, dissenters, and opponents. Many defenders of minorities accordingly aim to "sell" the minority to the majority. Gandhi made the same mistake. Lionel Curtis, the head of the Transvaal Republic's Asiatic Department, newly created to deal with the problem of Indians, reports that Gandhi came to see him and "started by trying to convince me of the good points in the character of his countrymen, their industry, frugality, their patience."

"Mr. Gandhi," Curtis says he replied, "you are preaching to the converted. It is not the vices of Indians that Europeans in this country fear but their virtues." And since, in other situations, vices are given as the excuse for discrimination, neither the virtues nor vices are decisive; discrimination requires a cure of the discriminators. Gandhi undertook that too. By purifying the oppressors as well as the oppressed he hoped to contribute to man's moral progress.

Gandhi recognized that the whites in South Africa thought they needed protection against a majority consisting of Negroes and Indians. The province of Natal, in 1896, had 400,000 Negro inhabitants, 51,000 Indians, and 50,000 whites. The Cape of Good Hope Colony had 900,-000 Negroes, 10,000 Indians, and 400,000 Europeans; the

Transvaal Republic 650,000 Negroes, 5,000 Indians, and
120,000 whites. In 1914, the five million Negroes hope-
lessly outnumbered the million and a quarter whites.

Apparently the whites were afraid that the Indians would
supply the Negroes with leadership. Or maybe the Indians,
being immigrants and fewer than the Negroes, were an
easier target.

Indians began coming into South Africa in 1860 as
indentured laborers imported to till the British-owned
sugar, tea, and coffee plantations where Negroes were reluctant to work. They came as term serfs for a period of five
years. Sometimes they remained as free workingmen for
five more years. In either case, the contractor paid their
passage back to India. Frequently, however, the indentured
laborers found conditions better than in India and chose to
remain in South Africa as free men. Disturbed by the growing number of Indian residents and by their affluence, for
they were hard-working, able, and thrifty, the whites
changed the regulations in 1894; thenceforth an indentured
person had to return to India at the expiration of his first
five-year term of service or become a serf in South Africa
for life. An escape clause provided that he might remain as
a free workingman by paying an annual tax of three pounds
for himself and each of his dependents, but since this was
prohibitively high, the real alternatives were repatriation
or permanent slavery.

Free immigrants also made their way from India to South
Africa and earned their livelihood as hawkers, tradesmen,
artisans, and professional men like Gandhi. Some acquired
considerable property. Indians even owned steamship lines.

These free Indians were subjects of Her British Majesty,
Queen Victoria, and those who could meet the wealth
qualifications (250, to be exact) were entitled to vote. In
1894, a year after Gandhi's first arrival in South Africa,
the Natal legislature passed a law explicitly disfranchising
Asiatics.

Many disabilities rested on Indians: in Natal province
an Indian had to carry a pass if he appeared on the streets
after 9 P.M. The Orange Free State, a republic set up by
the Boers, or Dutch settlers, forbade Indians to own property, to engage in trade, or to farm. In the Crown Colony
of Zululand, Indians were forbidden to buy or own land.

In Transvaal, too, Indians had no right to own land and, in addition, they had to pay a three-pound tax for a residence permit—but residence was limited to the slums. Some communities in Cape Colony prohibited Indians from walking on pavements. Even where no such restrictions existed Indians avoided the sidewalks because they might be kicked off. Gandhi was once kicked. Yet statute books described Indians as "semi-barbarous Asiatics."

"They treat us as beasts," Gandhi exclaimed at a meeting in Madras, on October 26, 1896, during a brief visit to his native land.

The Boer War having been waged from 1899 to 1902 between the Dutch settlers and the British and won by the latter, both sides proceeded to heal their wounds, as is frequently the case, with the balm of a third party's misery. The Indian question in South Africa consequently became a political football. Jan Christiaan Smuts, a Boer general and lawyer, who, after the Boer defeat, became Minister of Finance and Defense of South Africa, declared in an election speech in October, 1906, "The Asiatic cancer, which has already eaten so deeply into the vitals of South Africa, ought to be resolutely eradicated." General Louis Botha, likewise a former Boer general, and now Prime Minister, made the government's anti-Indian plan more specific; in January, 1907, at an electoral rally, he asserted, "If my party is returned to office we will undertake to drive the coolies out of the country within four years." "Coolies" was an insulting term applied to Indians.

The existence of more than one hundred thousand Indians was in jeopardy. Gandhi believed he could save them.

# 6 Courage Under Attack

Gandhi did not expect to eradicate white prejudices. "Prejudices," he wrote in the *Times of India* of June 2, 1918, "cannot be removed by legislation. . . . They yield only to patient toil and education." Nor did he hope to end segregation quickly. The Indians, he declared, "feel the ostracism but they silently bear it." His quarrel with the South Africans was "for feeding the prejudice by legalizing

it." At least the laws must be just, he pleaded. He did not
anticipate fair administration of the laws; the whites would
always be favored. But once the principle of legal equality
was established he would be content to let life work out its
complicated pattern and trust good citizens to brighten it.
If, however, the Indians supinely accepted their "inferiority" they would lose dignity and deteriorate morally. So
would the whites who imposed the inferiority.

Having been away from his family and Indian home for
three years, and realizing that his antidiscrimination work
would require his presence in South Africa for an extended
period, Gandhi returned to India in 1896 to fetch Kasturbai, Harilal, who was now eight, and a second son, Manilal,
born on October 28, 1892. He used the opportunity to
inform his countrymen on the plight of their brethren in
South Africa. These activities, reported back to South
Africa, stirred such bitter resentment that when his ship
docked at Durban (a second boat arrived from India at the
same time and both carried eight hundred passengers)
Gandhi was accused of flooding the country with unwanted
Indians. Actually he had nothing to do with their coming.
The whites demanded that both steamers return to India
with their human cargo. When finally the passengers were
allowed to disembark, Gandhi was attacked by a hostile
crowd. Stones, bricks, and eggs were hurled at him, his
turban was torn off his head, and he was beaten and kicked.
He fainted from pain but caught hold of the iron railing of
a house and remained erect. White men continued to smack
his face and strike his body. At this moment, Mrs. Alexander, wife of the municipal police superintendent, happened to pass and placed herself between the maddened
mob and the miserable Gandhi. Bruised and bleeding, he
was taken to the home of a friendly Indian to which Mrs.
Gandhi and the two boys had gone. Howling gangs surrounded the house and demanded that Gandhi be surrendered to them. Now Mr. Alexander came on the scene.
The multitude wanted Gandhi's blood. "We'll burn him,"
they shouted. At calmer intervals they sang, "And we'll
hang old Gandhi on the sour apple tree." Some prepared to
set fire to the house. Alarmed, the police superintendent
secretly sent two detectives into the house. One of them
gave Gandhi his uniform and helmet and then both con-

stables daubed their skin and dressed like Indians. Thus
disguised they escaped through the rear of the house and,
threading their way through side streets, deposited Gandhi
in the police station where he stayed for three days until
tempers subsided.

When news of this frustrated lynching reached London,
Joseph Chamberlain, the British Secretary of State for
Colonies, instructed the Natal authorities to put the at-
tackers on trial. Gandhi knew several of his assailants but
he refused to move against them. He said it was not their
fault, it was the fault of the community and the government, and he would not prosecute. "This is a religious question with me," he declared, and he would exercise "self-
restraint."

Two years later, Gandhi volunteered to raise a corps of
Indian stretcher-bearers and medical orderlies for the
British side in the Boer war. The Natal government spurned
the offer. Nevertheless, Gandhi and other Indians began,
at their own expense, to train as nurses. The government
again refused to avail itself of the Indians' services. But the
Boers were advancing, the dead were piling up on the
battlefields and the wounded lacked adequate care. Finally
the authorities sanctioned the formation of an Indian Ambulance Corps. Three hundred free Indians enlisted as well
as eight hundred indentured laborers furloughed by their
masters. South Africa and England rewarded them with
applause to which, when they heard about the Indians'
courageous behavior under fire, admiration was added.

In the Johannesburg *Illustrated Star* of July, 1911, Mr.
Vere Stent, a British editor, wrote an article about the
sanguinary engagement at Spion Kop in January, 1900.
General Buller, the British commander, was being pushed
back and he sent through an urgent dispatch asking that the
Indians rescue the wounded. Gandhi led his men on to the
battlefield. For days, under the fire of enemy guns, they
carried moaning soldiers to the base hospital. "After a
night's work which had shattered men with much bigger
frames," Mr. Stent recalled, "I came across Gandhi in the
early morning sitting by the roadside eating a regulation
army biscuit. Every man in Buller's force was dull and
depressed, and damnation was invoked on everything. But
Gandhi was stoical in his bearing, cheerful, and confident

in his conversations, and had a kindly eye. He did one good." He wore a khaki uniform, a jaunty, broad-brimmed cowboy felt hat, a Red Cross armband, and a drooping mustache. When the corps was disbanded it was mentioned in dispatches and Gandhi and several comrades were awarded the War Medal.

Gandhi had hoped that the fortitude of the Indians in war would appeal to the South Africans' sense of fair play and moderate white hostility to colored Asiatics. Instead, tension waxed. Nevertheless Gandhi again joined the British army with a platoon of twenty-four Indian stretcher-bearers and sanitary aids when the Zulu "rebellion" began in the first half of 1906. He volunteered, he said, because "the British Empire existed for the welfare of the world" and he had a "genuine sense of loyalty" to it.

During these years in South Africa and the intervals he spent in India, Gandhi displayed unflagging energy, an inexhaustible capacity for indignation, honesty which inspired trust, and a talent for easy personal relations with the lowly and mighty. He had proved himself an excellent organizer and effective leader. The great Gandhi of history, however, was only germinating and as yet gave little visible evidence of the fact.

## 7  The Transformation

In South Africa, Gandhi wore a European suit, stiff white wing collar and stiff white shirt, a gay striped necktie, and brightly polished shoes. At Durban, he rented an English villa in a fashionable part of the beach. He was earning five to six thousand pounds annually, or twenty-five to thirty thousand dollars, from legal work, and on the whole his life resembled that of an Indian Europeanized by constant imitation of the white world.

But he had strange ideas. When Ramdas, his third son, was born in South Africa in 1897, he took charge of the infant, and having studied a book on obstetrics entitled *Advice to a Mother,* he delivered his fourth son, Devadas, on May 22, 1900. "I was not nervous," he reported.

He must have been an unmitigated nuisance to Kasturbai

in the household. Not only did he interfere in the kitchen and nursery, he generously invited in a lot of unpaid boarders, performed menial tasks for them, and forced Kasturbai to do likewise. There was no running water in the Gandhi home; each room had a chamber pot. Gandhi refused to employ an untouchable or "sweeper" who in India does all the "unclean" jobs. He and Kasturbai, and sometimes the older boys, carried out the pots. He insisted; she had no choice. But one boarder, a clerk in Gandhi's law office, was a former untouchable who became a Christian to escape the ugly disabilities which Hindus inflict on their "outcastes." To the orthodox Kasturbai, however, he was still an untouchable and she balked at cleaning his pot. In fact, she hated the whole business and did not see why she, or for that matter her husband and children, should be doing these things. He, however, considered it part of her education, and sometimes she cried her eyes red. This riled him. Not only must she do the chores, she must do them cheerfully, and when he saw her weep, he shouted—as he himself tells the story: "I will not have this nonsense in my house." "Keep your house to yourself and let me go," she exclaimed.

Gandhi grabbed her by the hand, dragged her to the gate, opened it, and was about to push her out. "Have you no shame?" she sobbed. "Where am I to go? I have no parents or relatives here. For Heaven's sake, behave yourself and shut the gate. Let us not be found making scenes like this."

This brought him to his senses. He had a violent nature and his subsequent mahatma-calm was the product of long training in temperament-control. He did not easily become an evenminded, desireless yogi. He had to remold himself. Recognizing his deficiencies, he made a conscious effort to grow and change and restrain his bad impulses. He turned himself into a different person. He was a remarkable case of second birth in one lifetime. The transformation began in South Africa, and the result was a self-remade man.

In 1896, on the eve of a trip to India, the Indian community in South Africa had given him many personal gifts which he accepted without qualms. But when a treasure of jewels, including a gold necklace for Kasturbai, was presented to him in 1901 as he was planning to return to Bombay, he spent a sleepless night torn between a yearning for security, which the little heap of diamonds, pearls, rubies and gold trinkets would have brought him, and the desire to achieve freedom by owning less. Finally he decided to give up the jewelry. Kasturbai's protest availed nothing. The gifts were used to create a trust fund for South African Indians.

In Bombay, in 1901, an American insurance agent called on Gandhi to sell him a policy. The man, says Gandhi, had a "pleasant countenance" and "a sweet tongue." He discussed Gandhi's future "as though we were old friends." In America, the agent declared, "a person like you would always carry insurance; life is uncertain." Then, finding Gandhi's Achilles heel, the agent declared, "It's your religious duty to be insured." Gandhi was inclined to trust God rather than an insurance company, but the glib American shook the future Mahatma's faith and carried off a five-thousand-dollar policy.

Two years later, back in South Africa, Gandhi changed his mind. He used to devote thirty-five minutes to his morning toilet, twenty minutes for bathing and "fifteen minutes for the toothbrush," an old Indian custom, and during this prolonged oral massage, he memorized the *Bhagavad-Gita.* Impressed again, by its doctrine of "non-possession," he let the insurance policy lapse. "God would take care" of the family. The transformation was under way.

About this time Gandhi became acquainted with a British vegetarian, Henry S. L. Polak, assistant editor of the *Transvaal Critic.* One evening, when Gandhi was taking a train, Polak lent him a copy of *Unto This Last* by John Ruskin, English essayist and art critic. Gandhi sat up all night reading it. "That book," he said in October, 1946, "marked the turning point in my life." Straightaway, he decided to settle on a farm and live simply. Nothing in the volume need have suggested such a course. It is merely that Gandhi was ready for a back-to-nature move and a passage in Ruskin crystallized his determination. He frequently read into texts what he wanted them to say. A creative reader, he co-authored the impression a book made on him. He put things into it and took them back with interest. "It was a habit with me," he once wrote, "to forget what I did not like and to carry out in practice what I liked."

Having read Gandhi into Ruskin, Gandhi immediately bought a hundred-acre farm near Phoenix, Natal, for a thousand pounds and transferred to it the presses and editorial office of the weekly magazine, *Indian Opinion,* which he had taken over several months earlier. He and the family lived now in Johannesburg, where he pursued his large law practice, now at Phoenix Farm, where all hands helped to print the paper and cultivate the mango and orange trees.

The problem of austerity and self-control occupied Gandhi increasingly. He took to fasting, like his mother, whenever an occasion arose, and on other days he subsisted on two meager meals of nuts and fruits without spices or seasoning. On the farm he inaugurated his lifelong search for a diet which, while sustaining animal man, lifted the mind above the animal. We live, he felt, not in order to feed, clothe, shelter and pamper the body; we provide for the body in order to live. Life begins after the needs of the body have been met, yet how many people ruin life for the sake of rich living. The soul, alas, needs a temporary abode, but a clean mud hut will do as well as a palace, indeed better, for when the physical absorbs the lion's share of man's effort the spirit languishes, life loses content, and discontent appears.

The renunciation of pleasures is masochism, a Westerner says. Yet the Christian ethic is ascetic, and sainthood in all religions is related to self-denial. Gandhi did not believe in renunciation for its own sake or to torment the flesh. "A mother," he wrote in a letter, "would never by choice sleep in a wet bed but she would gladly do so in order to spare the dry bed for her child." Gandhi's renunciation was the unselfishness of love. Everyone experiences glorious moments of identification, through love, with his fellows. A saint has many such moments when, instead of being preoccupied with his person, he forgets and transcends it and occupies a place inside others. That union effaces at least a part of the gulf between mine and thine and thereby creates strength with happiness. At the height of his mahatmahood Gandhi was capable of a considerable degree of spiritual implantation in his followers. Any documentary film of Gandhi in India shows his almost total unawareness of self and oneness with others in contrast to the self-consciousness and conspicuous stage mannerisms of the lesser politician. This is a secret of his greatness and influence; he merged with those who surrounded him. The phenomenon had an enormous emotional impact on all, friend and foe, who beheld it and often vanquished their resistance even though the means by which he achieved it had excited doubt or revulsion. They might dislike what he did but could not withstand what he was as a result of doing it.

One of the things he did was to give up sex. During treks from village to village at the time of the Zulu insurrection, he indulged in long periods of introspection and finally decided to abstain from sexual intercourse forever. Twice before, he tells us quite simply, he had tried to become continent. Kasturbai agreed. They began sleeping in separate beds, and he never retired until physically exhausted. Both times, however, he succumbed.

But while up in Zululand he took a vow and that made it final. On demobilization he went to Phoenix Farm and told Kasturbai about his resolution. She made no protest. "She was never the temptress," he wrote. The nature of their intimate relations had been determined by him.

Gandhi remained celibate from 1906, when he was thirty-seven, until his death in 1948.

It is difficult to plumb Gandhi's motives; even he did not know them. He believed his celibacy was "a response to the call of public duty." On the other hand, "My main object was to escape having more children." But why avoid additional children? Phoenix Farm had become a sort of community project into which he invited numerous children and adults whose care was a common responsibility and expense. Why not more of his own?

Gandhi's celibacy is further complicated by what appears to have been a sense of guilt about sex. He was massaging his father Karamchand's legs one evening, he tells us, when, his passion aroused, he asked his uncle to relieve him and went to Kasturbai's bed. In a few minutes a servant knocked and summoned Gandhi. But when he reached the sickroom his father was dead. "If passion had not blinded me," Gandhi ruminated forty years later, "I should have been spared the torture of separation from my father during his last moments. . . . The shame of my carnal desire at the critical moment of my father's death . . . is a blot I shall never be able to efface or forget." It must have influenced his subsequent conduct. He called his thirty-three months' stay in London "a long and healthy separation from Kasturbai. On first leaving for South Africa he told her, "by way of consolation," "We are bound to meet again in a year." He was absent three years.

Celibacy, or Bramacharya, is encountered frequently in Hindu lore and life. Having performed his reproductive duty to family, caste and country, the Hindu may, in his fifties or late forties, graduate into extramarital unproductive sex or none, but it is unusual for a man to become a Brahmachari at the early age at which Gandhi took the vow. Perhaps he felt that four sons were duty enough. Or, fatherhood was sinful because he thought he had sinned at the moment of his father's death. Kasturbai's condition may also have contributed. She was anemic and was once near death from internal hemorrhage; a gynecological operation, performed without chloroform because she was so emaciated, brought relief but no cure. Her physiology perhaps faced him with—in his case—the obvious choice between infidelity and chastity.

In retrospect, in any event, he identified the motive with the effect and the effect was spiritual. Bramacharya, "fully and properly understood," he wrote in 1924, "means search after Brahma," or God. It "signifies control of all the senses at all times and all places in thought, word, and deed." It includes yet transcends sexual restraint; it embraces restraint in diet, emotions, and speech. It rules out violence, untruth, hate and anger. It creates evenmindedness. It is desirelessness. "Perfect Brahmacharis," Gandhi assumed, "are perfectly sinless. They are therefore near to God. They are like God." To that he aspired. It was the ultimate in self-transformation.

In renunciation, it is not the comforts, luxuries and pleasures that are hard to give up. Many could forgo heavy meals, a full wardrobe, a fine house, etcetera; it is the ego that they cannot forgo. The self that is wrapped, suffocated, in material things—which include social position, popularity, and power—is the only self they know and they will not abandon it for an illusory new self, for a different life, shorn of material trappings, which they may never attain, which perhaps does not exist, not for them, at any rate, and not in their surroundings. Gandhi, however, had the courage

to jump from the solid ground of his old self into the un-
known where, by some unfathomable endowment, he knew
he could find a shelf from which to move his world. It was
not easy. It must have been physically painful. He was
powerfully sexed; women attracted him even after his vow.
He had a "capacious stomach," he said, and a strong appe-
tite. He was earning well and might have become a very
rich lawyer. Voluntary celibacy and poverty, therefore,
represented hardships. He could endure them, indeed invite them, because he believed in something strongly, he
had a cause. With faith, renunciation is no sacrifice, it
substitutes one pleasure for another. Some give a dona-
tion, Gandhi gave himself—and found himself. The amount
of giving is determined by the intensity of belief. "Only
give up a thing," Gandhi wrote, "when you want some
other condition so much that the thing has no longer any
attraction for you, or when it seems to interfere with that
which is more greatly desired."

The chaste, austere life constituted a form of sublimation
which reinforced Gandhi's social passions. Renunciation
redoubled his desire to work for the common welfare. Less
carnal, he became less self-centered. By lifting himself
above the material he freed himself to work more fully for
his ideals. Greater control over self gave him greater control
over others. To be sure, storms continued to rage within
him, but now he could harness them for the generation of
more public power.

Renunciation had one direct additional advantage: people trusted him more. Perhaps because they have been ex-
ploited and abused for centuries and left helplessly dependent on their own meager resources, Indians often suspect
persons bringing gifts. They suspect self-interest and fear a
trap. They find it difficult to believe that anybody would
give something for nothing. They have experienced too
many situations in which the rich and mighty merely took.
For this reason, once they are completely convinced of a
person's unselfishness, they deluge him with unbridled devotion and slavish obedience. That was Gandhi's reward.

Stronger in himself and his following, the new Gandhi
faced the South African government. For the next eight
years he wrestled with it and in the end he won.

Henry Polak quotes Gandhi as remarking in South Africa, "Men say I am a saint losing myself in politics. The fact is I am a politician trying my hardest to be a saint." Actually Gandhi's politics are indistinguishable from his religion. "My patriotism," he said, "is subservient to my religion." In politics he cleaved to moral considerations, and as a saint he thought his place was not in a cave or cloister but in the hurly-burly of the popular struggle for rights and the right. Gandhi's religion made him political, and his politics were religious.

Saintly politician or political saint, and with all the added effectiveness which renunciation gave him, Gandhi could never have achieved what he did in South Africa and India but for a weapon peculiarly his own. It was unprecedented and has remained unimitated, indeed it was so unique he could not find a name for it until he finally hit upon "Satyagraha": *satya* means truth, the equivalent of love, and both are attributes of the soul; *agraha* is firmness or force. "Satyagraha" is therefore translated Soul Force.

Satyagraha, Gandhi wrote, "is the vindication of truth not by infliction of suffering on the opponent but on one's self." The opponent must be "weaned from error by patience and sympathy." Weaned, not crushed. Satyagraha assumes a constant beneficent interaction between contestants with a view to their ultimate reconciliation. Violence, insults, and superheated propaganda obstruct this end.

Gandhi never sought to humiliate or defeat the whites in South Africa or the British in India. He wished to convert them. He hoped that if he practiced the Sermon on the Mount, General Jan Christiaan Smuts would remember he was a Christian.

Satyagraha reverses the eye-for-an-eye-for-on-eye-for-an-eye policy which ends in making everybody blind or blind with fury. It returns good for evil until the evildoer tires of evil. In South Africa and at times in India Gandhi showed that ordinary human beings were capable of high-mindedness even under very irritating circumstances.

Satyagraha received its first test when the *Transvaal Government Gazette* of August 22, 1906, published the draft of an act requiring all Indian men and women, and children above the age of eight to submit to official registration and fingerprinting on pain of fines, imprisonment, and deportation from the province. The same penalties would be inflicted on any Indian found without a certificate of registration.

Gandhi told a mass meeting in the Imperial Theatre of Johannesburg on September 11, 1906, that this law was directed against Indians and was therefore an affront to them and India. "The government," he asserted, "has taken leave of all sense of decency," and he called on the audience of three thousand to pledge defiance of the ordinance and go to jail or, if need be, die. He warned them that the struggle would be long, "But," he emphasized, "I can boldly declare and with certainty that so long as there is even a handful of men true to their pledge, there can be only one end to the struggle—and that is victory." This was one of the basic principles of Satyagraha: Soul Force does not depend on numbers. It depends on the degree of firmness.

The Asiatic Registration Act was passed on July 31, 1907. Gandhi, affirming that "even a crooked policy would in time turn straight if only we are true to ourselves," led his countrymen in refusing to register. He was sentenced to two months' imprisonment. Before long, an emissary from General Smuts came to the jail with an offer to repeal the act if the Indians registered voluntarily. Gandhi was conducted to Smuts's office where, in prison uniform, he discussed and accepted the proposal. He and the other Indians were then released.

Returned to Johannesburg, Gandhi encountered fierce opposition from Indians who said the act should be revoked first, before the registration. "What if Smuts breaks faith with us?" they demanded.

"A Satyagrahi," he replied, "bids good-by to fear. He is therefore never afraid to trust the opponent. Even if the opponent plays him false twenty times, the Satyagrahi is ready to trust him the twenty-first time, for an implicit trust in human nature is the very essence of his creed." He then explained his readiness to compromise on voluntary registration: To bow to compulsion reduces the individual's dignity and stature, but the government's difficulties had to be considered; it was under strong pressure from race-conscious whites. Registration was designed to keep Indians from entering Transvaal illegally, and, Gandhi declared, since they did not intend bringing immigrants into the province "surreptitiously or by fraud," why not register? Collaboration freely given was generous and hence ennobling. Therefore the withdrawal of compulsory registration altered the situation.

At the meeting where these remarks were made, a giant Pathan from the wild mountains of northwest India near the Khyber Pass arose and shouted, "We will never give the fingerprints nor allow others to do so. I swear with Allah as my witness that I will kill the man who takes the lead in applying for registration."

Gandhi answered that he would be the first to register. "Death," he added, "is the appointed end of all life. To die by the hand of a brother, rather than by disease or in such other way, cannot be for me a matter of sorrow. And if, even in such a case, I am free from the thought of anger or hatred against my assailant, I know that it will redound to my eternal welfare, and even the assailant will later on realize my perfect innocence." No one could have foreseen that forty-two years later Gandhi would die at the hand of a brother. The Pathan kept his word. As Gandhi was proceeding to the registration office, Mir Alam, six feet tall and of powerful build, advanced upon Gandhi and struck him heavily on the head. "I at once fainted with the words 'Hey, Rama (Oh, God)' on my lips" reads Gandhi's own account. Murmuring these same words he was to die on January 30, 1948.

Mir Alam was arrested with other Pathans, but Gandhi obtained their release. "They thought they were doing right," he said, "and I have no desire to prosecute them."

On recovering from the attack, Gandhi registered and many Indians followed his example. What was his embarrassment, therefore, when Smuts refused to fulfill his promise to repeal the compulsory registration act. "There you are," Indians taunted Gandhi. "We have been telling you that you are very credulous."

At 4 o'clock on August 16, 1908, more than two thousand Indians congregated in the Hamidia Mosque in Johannesburg and threw their registration certificates into a huge cauldron filled with burning paraffin. The correspondent of the London *Daily Mail* compared it to the Boston Tea Party.

Gandhi's law offices in Johannesburg now became the
G.H.Q. of the Satyagraha movement. At other times he
stayed on Phoenix Farm, in Natal, soliciting support from
the Indians of that province, who far outnumbered the
thirteen thousand in Transvaal. On the farm, he led a
frugal, Spartan existence, sleeping in the open, except when
it rained, on a thin cloth. He eschewed material pleasures
and concentrated on the coming battle. "A Satyagrahi," he
wrote, "has to be, if possible, even more single-minded than
a rope dancer." He was in training for the moral fight. The
issue was now joined: the Indians had decided to defy the
ban on Indian immigration into the Transvaal and to court
arrest by circulating without registration certificates.

Presently Gandhi made a move of dramatic simplicity.
Indians in Natal had been asking him to let them test the
Transvaal immigration ban. He chose one and then another
and then more, including his eldest son, Harilal, to appear
peacefully at the Transvaal frontier post and try to enter.
Each was arrested and given three months in jail. Gandhi
joined them. So did scores of Indians in Transvaal who told
the police they had no certificates.

Gandhi became the cook for seventy-five of his compatriots in one prison. He also performed hard labor which
blistered his hands, and volunteered to clean the toilets.
"The real road to happiness," Gandhi wrote in a contem-
porary article, "lies in going to jail and undergoing suffering
and privations there in the interest of one's country and
religion." The prisoner's soul, he found, was free. In this
he echoed Henry David Thoreau, the New England rebel,
who wrote of his own prison experience, "I did not feel
for a moment confined, and the walls seemed a great waste
of stone and mortar." Gandhi copied these words from
Thoreau's "Civil Disobedience" and studied the entire essay
during his second stay in jail. He called it a "masterly
treatise" which "left a deep impression on me." There was
a Thoreau imprint on much that Gandhi did, as there was
an Indian imprint on Thoreau; he and his friend Ralph
Waldo Emerson had read the *Bhagavad-Gita* and some of
the sacred Hindu *Upanishads*. Thus Thoreau in Massachusetts borrowed from Gandhi's India and repaid the debt
with words that reached Gandhi in a South African cell.

"The only obligation which I have the right to assume,"

Thoreau said in "Civil Disobedience," "is to do at any time what I think right." He felt it more honorable to be right than to be law-abiding. He was writing in 1849 in protest against slavery and the invasion of Mexico. "There are thousands who are *in opinion* opposed to slavery and war," he declared, "who yet do nothing to put an end to them. There are nine hundred and ninety-nine patrons of virtue to every virtuous man."

Like Gandhi, Thoreau believed in the ability of the determined moral minority to correct the evils of the majority. "I know this well," Thoreau wrote, "that if one thousand, if one hundred, if ten men whom I could name—if ten *honest* men only—ay, if one HONEST man, in this state of Massachusetts, *ceasing to hold slaves,* were actually to withdraw from this copartnership [with the government] and be locked up in the county jail therefor, it would be the abolition of slavery in America. For it matters not how small the beginning may seem to be: what is once well done is done forever. But we love better to talk about it. . . ."

Thoreau himself refused to pay taxes and was clapped into jail, but a friend paid for him and he came out in twenty-four hours. Emerson declared in his Essay on Politics, "I do not recall a single human being who has steadily denied the authority of the laws on the simple ground of his moral nature." Emerson died in 1882 and could not have known Gandhi who, at the very moment when he read Thoreau, was in jail for denying unjust laws on moral grounds and would do so steadily for the rest of his life.

Count Leo Tolstoy, with whom Gandhi corresponded in 1909 and 1910, had the same faith in the power of the moral individual and in civil disobedience. "The position of governments in the presence of men who profess Christianity," Tolstoy wrote in *The Kingdom of God Is Within You,* "is so precarious that very little is needed to shake their power to pieces." He defined a Christian: he "enters into no dispute with his neighbor, he neither attacks nor uses violence; on the contrary, he suffers himself, without resistance, and by his very attitude toward evil not only sets himself free, but helps to free the world at large from all outward authority."

Through manual labor, renunciation of property, austerity, and Christian preaching, Tolstoy tried, in his late years, to create a synthesis between religion and conduct. Thoreau too, and Ruskin, sought a closer correspondence between man's goals and man's acts. The artist in them strived for the integrity which comes from the integration of words with beliefs and of both with works.

Romain Rolland, who had come under the influence of Tolstoy, made a shrewd comparison between Tolstoy and Gandhi. "With Gandhi," Rolland wrote in 1924, "everything is nature, modest, simple, pure—while all his struggles are hallowed by religious serenity, whereas with Tolstoy everything is proud revolt against pride, hatred against hatred, passion against passion. Everything in Tolstoy is violence, even his doctrine of nonviolence."

Tolstoy was storm-tossed, Gandhi calm and equable. In this respect many associates of Gandhi were really Tolstoyans. By doing at all moments what he thought right and not what he thought expedient, or comfortable, or profitable, or popular, or safe, or impressive, Gandhi eliminated the conflicts in his personality and thereby acquired the power to engage in patient, peaceful conflicts with those whom he regarded as doing wrong. He took words and ideas seriously and felt that having accepted a moral precept he had to live it. Then he could preach it. He preached what he practiced.

At the root of innumerable wrongs in our civilization is the discrepancy between word, creed and deed. It is the weakness of churches, states, parties, and persons. It gives men and institutions split personalities. Gandhi attempted to heal the split by establishing harmony in place of discrepancy, and as he progressively attained it he became happy, relaxed, and gay.

Gandhi had mental health because in him word, creed, and deed were one; he was integrated. That is the meaning of integrity. "The truth shall make you free"—and well. Through truth, Gandhi set himself free in order to go to jail.

## 9   Happy Victory

To get a jail sentence, a Transvaal Indian merely had to leave for Natal province and return home to Transvaal. This violated the immigration ban and was punished with one to three months in prison. Some Soul-Force resisters served eight prison terms, courting a new sentence the moment they had served the old one. At one time, of the thirteen thousand men, women, and children of Indian descent in Transvaal, twenty-five hundred were in jail, and six thousand had fled the state. No end was in sight.

In 1909, Gandhi sent Henry Polak to India and he himself sailed for England. He felt that resentful people and sensitive administrators in one part of an empire overwhelmingly colored could help in the struggle against color discrimination in another part. If India became South-Africa-conscious the Viceroy's concern would be communicated to London which, properly prodded, might restrain Smuts. This is the now-mature lobbying technique, then in its infancy.

Gandhi won the support of many liberals and enlightened imperialists in England. Though his trip was barren of immediate concrete results, he succeeded in making the South African Indian question a major imperial headache. Therein lay the seed of ultimate triumph.

Returned to South Africa at the end of 1909, Gandhi decided to create "a sort of co-operative commonwealth" in miniature where civil resisters "would be trained to live a new simple life in harmony with one another." The movement needed a home for dependents of imprisoned resisters and for resisters themselves in intervals between sentences. Accordingly Herman Kallenbach, the second-in-command of the Satyagraha movement, a tall, thickset, square-headed German Jew with a handlebar mustache and pince-nez, a rich architect, Buddhist, pugilist, wrestler, pupil of the famous Sandow, a man, in Gandhi's words, "of strong feelings, wide sympathies, and childlike simplicity," bought 1100 acres of land at Lawley, twenty-one miles from Johannesburg, and gave it to the resisters free. Gandhi called it The Tolstoy Farm. He and his family and Kallenbach came to live there.

"I prepare the bread that is required on the farm," Gandhi wrote to a friend in India. "The general opinion about it is that it is well made. We put in no yeast and no baking powder. We have just prepared some marmalade from the oranges grown on the farm. I have also learned to prepare caramel coffee. It can be given as a beverage even to babies."

Gandhi was baker and caramel and marmalade maker. Kallenbach taught him to make cabinets, chests of drawers, and school benches, as well as leather sandals. Gandhi likewise sewed jackets for his wife which, he boasted, she actually wore. He assisted in the cookhouse, kept the women from quarreling, and served as general manager. Occasionally, when he could not help attending to a law case, he left the farm at 2 A.M., walked the twenty-one miles to town, and returned on foot the same night. One day, he recalls, "I walked fifty miles."

Gandhi said his physical stamina came from pure living and healthy diet. He and Kallenbach avoided cooked food and limited themselves to a "fruitarian" menu of bananas, dates, lemons, oranges, peanuts and olive oil. Having read of the cruelties practiced in India to make cows and water buffaloes yield the maximum in milk, they gave up milk.

The population of the farm varied according to the number of Satyagrahis in jail; sometimes it amounted to over a hundred. Kallenbach shared with Gandhi the task of teaching the children religion, geography, history, arithmetic and so forth.

Gandhi's ideas on coeducation were flagrantly unconventional. He encouraged boys and girls, some of them adolescents, to bathe together at the spring. For the girls' safety, he was always present, and "My eyes followed the girls as a mother's eye follows a daughter." No doubt the boys' eyes followed too. At night, everybody slept on an open veranda, and the young folks grouped their beds around Gandhi. Sleeping places were only three feet apart, but Gandhi said the young people knew he loved them "with a mother's love," and hadn't he told them about self-restraint?

Inevitably there was an incident, involving a girl and two boys, whereupon Gandhi searched for a way "to sterilize the sinner's eye" of the males. The quest kept him awake all night, but in the morning he had it: he asked the girl to shave her head. She was shocked but he was irresistible and she finally agreed. He did the cutting.

Commenting on this episode years later, Gandhi explained his innocence by ignorance. But why was he ignorant? He dispelled some of the mystery by adding that his "faith and courage were at their highest in Tolstoy Farm." Boundless faith in himself sometimes blinded him to the hesitations, feelings, and frailties of his friends. He measured other people's capacities by his own zeal. It was the kind of blindness that blots out obstacles and leads to brave ventures.

Meanwhile, the resistance movement settled down to an in-and-out-of-jail routine relieved by austerity on the farm. Nothing much happened. Spirits often flagged, but not Gandhi's. When Gopal Krishna Gokhale, outstanding leader of the Indian nationalist movement in India, arrived in October, 1912, to survey the South African scene and sternly asked Gandhi for a list of the really reliable resisters, he put down sixty-six names but admitted that their number might drop to sixteen. These he called his "army of peace." Yet no matter how thin their ranks, Gandhi never flinched. The government, he was certain, would yield to Soul Force. Gokhale had great influence with the people of India and their British rulers. The new Union of South Africa government under Generals Botha and Smuts, hoping he would carry back a good impression, gave him a warm reception and every facility for touring the country. They also promised to lift the immigration ban and abolish the three-pound annual tax on liberated indentured laborers.

"I doubt it very much," Gandhi said when Gokhale reported this pledge. "You do not know the Ministers as I do."

Gandhi revered Gokhale, asserted that he "was like the Ganges in whose refreshing, holy waters one longed to bathe," and accepted him as his political *guru* or mentor, but he would not defer to the opinions of anyone, no matter how exalted or beloved, if he deemed them wrong. Gokhale regarded the Botha-Smuts promise as signalizing the end of the South African struggle. He accordingly told Gandhi to "return to India within twelve months, and I will not have any of your excuses." Gandhi, however, was stubborn, and Gokhale rebuked him, saying, "You will always have your own way." Yet on returning to Bombay, he told a Town Hall meeting in December, 1912, that "Gandhi has in him the marvelous spiritual power to turn ordinary men around him into heroes and martyrs." In Gandhi's presence, he added, one is "ashamed to do anything unworthy," indeed one is "afraid of thinking anything unworthy." Confronted by prominent men like Gokhale, Gandhi felt respect and humility, even awe, but, wrapped in these sentiments, he sometimes became impervious to their thoughts. He was diffident yet independent. Self-confidence filled him with exuberant energy and a radiance which no critic and of course no follower could resist.

Developments proved Gandhi right. Smuts soon announced in the House of Assembly that the European employers of contract labor in Natal would not permit the lifting of the three-pound tax on ex-serfs. This was considered a breach of the Botha-Smuts promise to Gokhale and masses of indentured and former indentured Indians volunteered for civil disobedience.

To the two issues, the tax and the ban on immigration, a third was added when a Justice of the Cape Colony Supreme Court ruled that only Christian marriages were legal. "Then I am not your wife," Kasturbai exclaimed with horror. In effect Hindu, Moslem, and Parsi marriages were invalidated, and Indian wives were concubines. Large numbers of women joined the active resisters.

Gandhi planned his campaign. As a first move, a group of Natal "sisters" were to court arrest by entering the Transvaal without permission, and simultaneously a group of Transvaal "sisters" would enter Natal. The Natal "sisters" were imprisoned; indignation flared and brought new recruits. The Transvaal "sisters," however, were not arrested. Obeying previous instructions, they proceeded to the Newcastle coal mines and urged the indentured Indian miners to go on strike. Thereupon the government arrested the women and gave each a three months' jail sentence. The strike spread. Gandhi went to Newcastle. The mine owners turned off the light and water in the company houses occupied by Indian strikers.

Believing the strike would last a long time, Gandhi advised the strikers to leave their compounds, taking blankets and some clothing with them, and pitch camp in the open. In a few days, approximately five thousand Indians were living under the sky.

Gandhi did not know what to do with them. How could he feed and house this multitude? He finally decided to march them into Transvaal and "see them safely deposited in jail." Before breaking up camp, however, he telegraphed the government saying it could arrest the "peace army" right away before they started for Transvaal. The government was not inclined to do him any such favor. A week later, Gandhi telephoned Smuts in Pretoria renewing the request for immediate jail confinement in Natal but offering to send the men back to the mines if the three-pound tax was revoked. Smuts' secretary said, "General Smuts will have nothing to do with you. You may do just as you please."

Gandhi now proposed to cross over from Natal into Transvaal and if, as he suspected, the Transvaal government too refused to open its jails to his "army," they would advance on Tolstoy Farm by eight day-marches of twenty miles each. While planning the invasion (food had to be shipped to every halt) he warned the resisters of impending hardships and pleaded with the fainthearted to go home.

At 6:30 on the morning of November 6, 1913, Gandhi counted his forces. There were 2,037 men, 127 women, and 57 children. "We offered prayers," Gandhi wrote, "and commenced to march in the name of God."

The police at the Transvaal border allowed the marchers to pass. Some of the women carried babies on their hips or backs. Most of the people were barefooted. They were a motley crowd speaking Tamil, Telugu, Gujarati, Hindi and other Indian languages and dressed in different Indian costumes but all loyal to the little peace general whose battle orders were: Do not resist arrest; submit to police flogging; conduct yourself morally and hygienically.

At the end of the first day, Gandhi was arrested but released on bail because of his responsibility for the marchers. On the second night he was again arrested, taken to a court, and freed. On the fourth night he was arrested and held. The trek to Tolstoy Farm continued without him.

The next morning, when they reached Balfour, the marchers were herded into waiting trains and transported back to the mines in Natal where they were forced into wire-enclosed stockades guarded by company employees sworn in as special constables. But they refused to descend to the coal face.

More indentured laborers left their work in sympathy

with the miners. The state regarded these men as slaves without the right to strike and sent soldiers to suppress them. In one place the military fired and killed and wounded several Indians.

Fifty thousand indentured laborers were now on strike; several thousand free Indians were in jail. The news was wired to India, which roared with protest. Lord Hardinge, the British Viceroy, in a strong speech at Madras, broke the rule of noninterference, trenchantly criticized the South African authorities, and demanded a commission of inquiry. The cables between India and London and between London and South Africa hummed with voluminous messages. On December 18, 1913, the government released Gandhi and Polak and Kallenbach, who had been arrested with him. "All of us," Gandhi commented, "were disappointed upon our release"; civil disobedience, once properly launched, needs no leaders.

At the same time, the South African government appointed a commission to inquire into the grievances of Indian residents. Gandhi immediately branded it "a packed body and intended to hoodwink the government and public opinion both of England and of India." Sir William Solomon, the commission's chairman, Gandhi stated, had "integrity and impartiality," but Mr. Ewald Esselen was prejudiced, and the third member, Colonel J. S. Wylie, had been one of the leaders in the frustrated lynching when the two steamers with eight hundred Indians arrived in Durban, in January, 1897. Gandhi proposed the addition to the commission of several Indians or pro-Indians.

Expecting difficulties, Gandhi prepared to fight. At one mass meeting he appeared in a knee-length white smock, an elongated loincloth, and sandals. He had abandoned western dress, he said, to mourn the miners killed during the strike. "Are you prepared to share the fate of those of our countrymen whom the cold stone is resting upon today?" he demanded.

"Yes, yes," the meeting vowed.

"I hope," he continued, "that every man, woman, and grown-up child will not consider their salaries, trades, or even families, or their own bodies." He expected *Gita*-like self-abnegation from common clay. He got it, for they were religious folk, and he emphasized that this struggle was "a struggle for human liberty, and therefore a struggle for religion."

Accordingly, when Smuts refused to change or expand the grievance commission, Gandhi announced that he and Indians who might wish to join him would march from Durban, Natal, on New Year's Day, 1914, and invite arrest.

While this ugly threat of a new Indian mass march hung over the government's head, the white employees of all South African railways went on strike. Gandhi immediately called off his march. Soul Force, he explained, never took advantage of the opponent's weaknesses, nor did it form unnatural alliances. Civil resisters hope to convince the brain and conquer the heart by self-suffering, sincerity, and chivalry, not to hurt, humble or embitter the adversary. Messages of approval and congratulation poured in on Gandhi from India, England, and South Africa. Smuts, busy with the railway strike (martial law had been proclaimed) nevertheless summoned Gandhi for a talk. The Indians warned Gandhi against deception and recalled the broken pledge of 1908 and the broken promise to Gokhale. In reply, he quoted a Sanskrit proverb: "Forgiveness is the ornament of the brave."

The talk between Smuts and Gandhi lengthened into negotiations. "Gandhi," Smuts said at one of their interviews, "this time we want no misunderstanding, we want no mental or other reservations, let all the cards be on the table." This friendly approach conduced to slow yet steady progress. Every passage and word of the impending agreement was dissected. Finally, on June 30, 1914, the two subtle men exchanged letters confirming the terms of their pact. The document, translated into the legal language of the Indian Relief Bill, was submitted to the Union Parliament in Cape Town and adopted in July in the "noncontroversial spirit" for which Smuts had pleaded.

By the terms of the settlement, the three-pound tax on former indentured Indian laborers was annulled and arrears canceled; Hindu, Moslem, and Parsi marriages were declared valid; Indians born in South Africa could enter the Cape Colony, but free movement between Union provinces was otherwise prohibited; indentured contract labor would cease arriving from India in 1920; free Indians, however, could continue to enter, and wives could come from India to join their husbands.

Feted at a dozen dinners, Gandhi called the new law "the Magna Charta" of South African Indians. A compromise, for Indians would still be "cooped up" in their provinces and could not hold land in Transvaal or buy gold anywhere, it nevertheless constituted a vindication of the principle of racial equality and removed the "racial taint." Above all, it was a victory for the Soul Force, "a force which," he wrote in *Indian Opinion*, "if it became universal, would revolutionize social ideals and do away with despotisms and the ever-growing militarism under which the nations of the West are groaning . . ."

His mission accomplished, tired but happy, Gandhi, accompanied by Mrs. Gandhi, beautiful in white sari with a gay flower design, and by Herman Kallenbach, sailed for England on July 18, 1914. Before leaving he sent General Smuts a gift of a pair of leather sandals he had made in prison. Smuts wore them on his farm near Pretoria until 1939 when, as a gesture of friendship, he returned them to Gandhi in India, saying, "I have worn these sandals for many a summer since then, even though I may feel that I am not worthy to stand in the shoes of so great a man." Such humor and generosity proved him worthy of Gandhi's mettle. Gandhi had not won a victory over Smuts, he had won Smuts over. The settlement came not when Smuts had no more strength to fight but when he had no more heart to fight. "You can't put twenty thousand Indians into jail," Smuts declared at the time. He was happy when the struggle ended. Writing in 1939, in a gracious contribution to a fat seventieth-birthday Gandhi memorial volume, Smuts, by then a world-famous statesman, said men like Gandhi "redeem us from a sense of commonplace and futility, and are an inspiration to us not to weary in well-doing. . . . It was my fate to be the antagonist of a man for whom even then I had the highest respect. . . . He never forgot the human background of the situation, never lost his temper or succumbed to hate, and preserved his gentle humor in the most trying situations. His manner and spirit even then, as well as later, contrasted markedly with the ruthless and brutal forcefulness which is in vogue in our day."

Writing about it twenty-five years later was easier than living through it. "I must frankly admit," the Smuts article

continued, "that his activities at the time were very trying
to me. . . . Gandhi showed a new technique. . . . His
method was deliberately to break the law, and to organize
his followers into a mass movement." Many of these were
imprisoned and "Gandhi himself received—what no doubt
he desired—a period of rest and quiet in jail. For him
everything went according to plan. For me—the defender
of law and order—there was the usual trying situation, the
odium of carrying out a law which had not strong popular
support, and finally the discomfiture when the law was
repealed."

It took three to make the victory in South Africa in
1914: First, Gandhi. In a 1914 tribute to Gandhi in
*Hibbert Journal,* Professor Gilbert Murray of Oxford
wrote: "Be careful in dealing with a man who cares nothing
for sensual pleasures, nothing for comfort or praise or
promotion, but is simply determined to do what he believes
to be right. He is a dangerous and uncomfortable enemy
because his body which you can always conquer gives you
so little purchase over his soul." That explains Gandhi's
part in the victory. Second, there were the Indian Satyagrahis, who recalled the heroes described in a poem by
Shelley which Gandhi once read to a Christian gathering
in India:

> Stand ye calm and resolute
> Like a forest close and mute,
> With folded arms and looks which are
> Weapons of unvanquished war.
>
> . . . . . .
>
> And if then the tyrants dare,
> Let them ride among you there,
> Slash, and stab, and maim and hew,—
> What they like, that let them do.
>
> With folded arms and steady eyes,
> And little fear, and less surprise,
> Look upon them as they slay,
> Till their rage has died away.

Third, there was Smuts. A dictator would not have hesitated
to imprison twenty thousand Indians, or, indeed, to shoot
them, and to jail or hang Gandhi. No democracy, no
Gandhi. Smuts helped to make Gandhi by not destroying
him. Gandhi increased the stature of Smuts.

# PART TWO
# Gandhi In India

*January 9, 1915—March 23, 1946*

## 10   Ears and Mouth Open

In India, Gandhi's spiritual qualities were quickly perceived. After his return in January, 1915, audiences at
meetings shouted "Mahatmaji," "Mahatmaji" (the suffix
"ji" connotes affection and respect), and some time later
the title of Mahatma was conferred on him by Rabindranath
Tagore, Nobel Prize winner for literature in 1913. "Great
Soul in peasant's garb," the poet wrote, and the crown sat
forever on the politician-saint's head.

Tagore and Gandhi were the outstanding Indians of the
first half of the twentieth century. They revered one another. Tagore wept at seeing India "the eternal ragpicker
at other people's dustbins," an emotion Gandhi shared,
and he prayed, as did the Mahatma, for "the magnificent
harmony of all human races." They were nationalists yet
internationalists, sentimentally inseparable, and soulmates
to the end. But they were also deeply different and waged
frequent verbal battles. Gandhi was frugal, Tagore prodigal;
Gandhi the emaciated ascetic with shaven head and face,
Tagore the large, white-maned, white-bearded, rich aristocrat-intellectual with visage of classic beauty; Gandhi the
rice field, Tagore the rose garden; Gandhi the general,
Tagore the herald; Gandhi the working arm, Tagore the
singing voice. Gandhi sat, so to speak, in a market place
crisscrossed by tens of millions of persons with their carts,
cares, wares, and thoughts, but he sat still and within him
there was peace. He would have suffocated in an ivory
tower or on an Olympian height, whereas Tagore said, "If
I hear a song, my sitar can catch the melody, and I can

join the chorus, for I am a singer. But in the mad clamor of the crowd, my voice is lost, and I become dizzy." "The suffering millions," Gandhi told Tagore, "ask one poem, invigorating food." Tagore gave them music. At Shantiniketan, Tagore's pupils sang and danced, wove garlands, and made life beautiful. When Gandhi arrived on a visit he persuaded the teachers and students to run the kitchen, collect the garbage, clean the toilets, and sweep the grounds. Tagore tolerantly acquiesced, saying, "The experiment contains the key to Swaraj," or home rule, but when Gandhi left, the experiment collapsed. Perhaps, since provincial origins are so important in India (as a result of linguistic gulfs and meager transportation), theirs was the difference between isolated Kathiawar and cosmopolitan Bengal. Tagore accepted the present and the West with its culture and machines, and emancipated himself from religion. But Gandhi's bloodstream was Hinduism, the past of India his inspiration, God his daily companion. In retrospect, he stands out as a reformer of Hinduism, somewhat like Buddha. He was of Hinduism yet against its deformations and, simultaneously, a product and critic of Western civilization. He loved the West and resisted its influence over India, loved his country and flayed its flaws. Ideologically, he stood with one foot in the individualism and nationalism of Europe's nineteenth century, and with the second in the remote age of Hindustan's glory and obscurantism. The two streams merged in him, and he endeavored to achieve the same synthesis in the Indian independence movement. He tried to turn it toward the best in the West, toward Thoreau, Emerson, Ruskin, Mazzini and the Utopian (not Marxist) socialists. From these he took his defense of man against the machine and intertwined it with the roots of Hinduism. Theirs too was his championship of the individual against the community which, however, found no counterpart in India's social customs.

Gandhi wanted a new Indian today, not just a free India tomorrow. To him, true freedom for India meant the emergence of a new, free, Indian individual. He believed, with Tagore, that India's shackles were self-made. Tagore wrote: "Prisoner, tell me who was it that brought this unbreakable chain? It was I, said the prisoner, who forged this chain very carefully."

Gandhi's unconventional ideas on Indian independence evolved very early and spontaneously in his own personality, for he expressed them before he had had much adult experience in India. They appeared in 1909 in his first book, *Hind Swaraj or Indian Home Rule,* written, with right and left hands, on the steamer coming back from a lobbying trip to England. He allowed it to be republished in 1921 without change, and, in an introduction to still another edition in 1938, he declared, "I have seen nothing to make me alter the views expanded in it." The seventy-six-page pamphlet, therefore, stands as his credo.

"Some Englishmen state that they took and hold India by the sword," Gandhi wrote. "Both statements are wrong. The sword is entirely useless for holding India. We alone keep them. . . . We like their commerce; they please us by their subtle methods and get what they want from us. . . . We strengthen their hold by quarreling amongst ourselves."

Then he formulated the principles which would govern his efforts through the decades. "If we act justly India will be free sooner," he asserted. "You will see, too, that if we shun every Englishman as an enemy, Home Rule will be delayed. But if we are just to them, we shall receive their support." He neither blamed nor reviled the British yet hoped that free India would be unlike British India. Some argued that India after liberation must resemble Japan with "our own navy, our army . . . our own splendor, and then will India's voice ring through the world." In other words, Gandhi replied, you want "English rule without the Englishman. You want the tiger's nature without the tiger. . . . You would make India English. . . . This is not the Swaraj I want."

Indian nationalists whom he had encountered in London scorned his preoccupation with the ethical and social future of free India. Their sole aim was to expel the British, as Mazzini and Garibaldi had expelled the foreign masters of Italy. Gandhi demurred: "If you believe that because Italians rule Italy the Italian nation is happy you are groping in darkness. . . . According to Mazzini [freedom] meant the whole of the Italian people, that is, its agriculturists. The Italy of Mazzini still remains in a state of slavery." He made the same point in a letter to Lord

Ampthill, former Governor of Madras, on October 9, 1909: "I should be uninterested in the fact as to who rules." The important consideration was how he ruled. Indian rulers might be no better than British rulers, any more than "an Indian Rockefeller would be better than an American Rockefeller." Gandhi looked beyond national freedom to social liberation. Thirty-eight years before independence, his seer's eye foresaw the problems which rack independent India today. Not the nationality of administrators interested him, but their methods and morality. This concern for the content of freedom, for the truth behind the façade, form, and flag, shaped his efforts from 1915 to January 30, 1948, and explains several enigmatic intervals when he abandoned the pursuit of the British to pursue a principle.

Gandhi aired these ideas during his first year in India. G. K. Gokhale, president of the Servants of India Society, had "commanded" him to spend that year with "his ears open but his mouth shut." At the many meetings, however, where grateful countrymen celebrated Gandhi's acts in South Africa, he naturally talked, talked in a weak, unimpressive, conversational tone. Some were disappointed. They had expected a new giant, the lion of a man who had defeated Smuts. Instead they saw a spare little figure in a ridiculously large turban and flapping loincloth who could scarcely make himself heard, who, to boot, was saying strange things. A photograph taken that first year shows him seated on a platform, heels on his thighs, nude but for a loincloth, making a speech while all around stood Indian politicians in European dress. He told them to shed those garments. How could leaders in Bond Street suits or Bombay coats and trousers reach the peasants' hearts; how could English-speaking orators touch their minds?

Peasants? But politicians had nothing to do with peasants. India's home-rulers and nationalists, and the Indian National Congress party, or Congress as it was usually called, were hoping to persuade the British to transfer part of their power to Indians. With this in view, they donned black cutaways and striped pants and read petitions in impeccable English to polite English bureaucrats. India's independence hall, they thought, would be papered with memorials addressed to a most gracious sovereign and the sovereign's satrap. Others, especially in tumultuous Bengal, trained their brown hands and burning big brown eyes to shoot those British bureaucrats.

Not by terror, Gandhi taught, and not by "prayers" to English governors couched, as Tagore put it, in the "correct grammatical whine," would freedom be won. "No paper contributions will ever give us self-government," he told an illustrious assemblage of notables and students at the opening of the Hindu University Central College in Benares, in February, 1916. "No amount of speeches will make us fit for self-government. It is only our conduct that will fit us for it." Many maharajas and rajas were in the audience giving "an exhibition of jewelry," he said "which made a most gorgeous show." "Strip yourselves of this jewelry and hold it in trust for your countrymen in India," he urged. But he did not expect them to do it. "Our salvation can come only through the farmer. Neither the lawyers, nor the doctors, nor the rich landlords are going to secure it."

Village uplift was Gandhi's First Freedom. Over 80 per cent of India lived in her villages, and they were poor, illiterate, diseased, discouraged. Peasant liberation from destitution could not be the achievement of the small upper class or a gift of the foreign power. The peasants had to win it. Gandhi craved for his country a psychological metamorphosis which would give it inner freedom and, then, inevitably, outer freedom, for once the people acquired individual dignity they would insist on better living and nobody would hold them in bondage.

Distances in India are great and communications poor. Few can read and few possess radios. Therefore the ear of India is big and sensitive. In 1916, the ear began to catch the voice of a man who was courageous and indiscreet, a little man who loved the poor and defended them to the face of the rich, a holy man. Gandhi was not yet a national figure. The hundreds of millions did not know him. But the fame of the new Mahatma was spreading. Power, possessions, elephants, jewels, armies, and policemen win India's obedience. Devotion wins its heart.

Now Gandhi sat in his *ashram*. In ancient India, ashrams were religious retreats for monks. Ashramites resigned from the world, and, contemplating themselves inside and out, waited for the end. Gandhi's ashram, however, remained in closest contact with the world. In fact, it became the navel of India. Indians contemplated it and began a new life.

"Satyagraha Ashram" was located first at Kochrab and then, permanently, at Sabarmati, across the Sabarmati River from the crowded city of Ahmedabad. There, rooted in the sand and soil and people of India, Gandhi grew to full stature. The ashram consisted of a group of low, white-washed huts in a grove of spreading trees. Below the compound is the river in which women pound their laundry on the flat stones and cows and buffaloes wade. All around, the scene is gently pastoral but near by are twisted masses of closely packed slum dwellings huddling under the ugly smokestacks of the Ahmedabad textile factories whose owners financed the ashram. Gandhi's room was about the size of a cell; its window had iron bars put there by a former occupant. Except for intervals in prison, Gandhi lived in that cell for sixteen years. Some of the most active leaders of the independence movement began their political careers at the feet of the Mahatma at Sabarmati. The population of the settlement fluctuated from 30 at the start to 230 at its maximum. They tended the fruit trees, spun, wove, planted grain, prayed, studied, and taught in the surrounding villages. An air of soft repose and tranquility still hovered over the ashram when I visited it in 1948, a decade and a half after Gandhi had moved elsewhere.

To this day, the Indian's heart aches for the lost glory of his country. Gandhi brought it balm. Some sought the illusion of strength by twisting the lion's tail, and the motion became a reflex action which persisted after the lion was gone. Gandhi did not often succumb to that temptation. Instead he sat amid the trees, prayerful and imperturbable, no longer aping the British gentleman but resembling a saint of antiquity and reminding the nation that it had seen many conquerors and conquered them by being true to itself. Gandhi restored India's confidence. The magic wand of his personality became the national ramrod.

India had had great men before Gandhi who dreamt and worked for national regeneration. They were luminous planets in a remote firmament, brilliant stars shedding light

on a few satellites. Gandhi was planted solidly in the earth.
He took sustenance from the people who walked on it and
in turn fructified them. He was of the people, by the people,
and for the people.

## II   Mahatma Gandhi and the British

Gandhi was neither a conforming Hindu nor a conforming
nationalist. No ism held him in its grip. He never hewed
to a line. He was independent, unpredictable, and hence
exciting to all and difficult for the British. "Do I contradict
myself?" he asked. "Consistency is a hobgoblin." He had
the rebel's courage to be true to himself today and different
tomorrow. "My aim," he once wrote, "is not to be consistent with my previous statement on a given question, but
to be consistent with the truth as it may present itself to
me at a given moment. The result is that I have grown from
truth to truth. . . ." His pacifism, like his social philos-
ophy, was a slow growth. In 1914, en route from South
Africa to India, he raised an Ambulance Corps of Indian
students to serve the British Army, and admitted self-
accusingly that, "Those who confine themselves to attending the wounded in battle cannot be absolved from the
guilt of war." In India, later, he urged Indians to support
the British war effort. "I discovered," he said in defense of
this unpopular stand, "that the British Empire had certain
ideals with which I have fallen in love, and one of those
ideals is that every subject of the British Empire has the
freest scope possible for his energy and honor. . . . I have
more than once said that that government is best which
governs least. I have found that it is possible for me to be
governed least under the British Empire. Hence my loyalty
to the British Empire."

In July, 1918, he recruited for the British Army in town
and country: "There can be no partnership between the
brave and the effeminate. We are regarded as a cowardly
people. If we want to become free from that reproach, we
must learn the use of arms."

The peasants in the villages heckled him. "You are a
votary of nonviolence," they said; "how can you ask us to
take up arms?"

"Partnership in the Empire is our definite goal," he replied. He wanted India to enjoy the status of Canada, Australia, New Zealand. The idea of full separation had not yet captured his mind and was far from most Indian nationalists. "If the Empire perishes, with it perish our cherished aspirations," he argued.

In 1942, I asked Gandhi about his prowar attitude during the First World War. "I had just returned from South Africa," he explained. "I hadn't yet found my feet. I was not sure of my ground." Since he was compromising his nationalism to stay within the empire, his compulsive honesty forced him to compromise his pacifism and recruit for the British Army. Realism triumphed over religion. Politics diluted his pacifism.

So far, he had had only one brush with the British. The episode commenced during the annual convention of the Indian National Congress in Lucknow, United Provinces, in December, 1916. "A peasant," Gandhi recounted, "came to me looking like any other peasant in India, poor and emaciated, and said, 'I am Rajkumar Shukla. I am from Champaran, and I want you to come to my district.'" Gandhi had never heard of the place; it lay in the foothills of the Himalayas in the state of Bihar, near the remote kingdom of Nepal.

The sharecroppers were having trouble with the British landlords. Would not Gandhi come to hear their grievances? the peasant asked. The Mahatma pleaded commitments in other parts. Shukla followed him everywhere and finally came to the ashram. For weeks he never left Gandhi's side. "Fix a date," he begged.

Impressed by the tenant's tenacity, Gandhi gave him an appointment in Calcutta several months hence. Shukla was sitting there on his haunches when Gandhi arrived and waited till he was free. Then they traveled to Champaran.

Gandhi took pains to ascertain all the facts. First, he visited the British landlords' association. The secretary told him he could give no information to an outsider. Gandhi said he was no outsider. Next, he called on the British commissioner who, Gandhi reports, "proceeded to bully me and advised me to leave . . ." He remained.

The situation, according to Gandhi's findings and subsequent historic research, was this: over a million peasants

cultivated land rented from Englishmen; they could grow
rice, wheat, corn, barley, or any crop they chose, but 15
per cent of their fields had to be sown with indigo and the
harvest paid to the estate owners as the rent for the entire
farm. In the early years of the twentieth century, however,
the dye industry in Germany had developed synthetic indigo
and the world market for natural-grown indigo collapsed.
The landlords thereupon ordered their sharecroppers to
plant no indigo and, simultaneously, increased the rent.
They did this under an old agreement which provided that
if a peasant gave up indigo cultivation his rent could be
raised. But the peasants had learned about synthetic indigo
and knew why the landlords wanted no indigo planted;
they therefore resisted the rent rise. The landlords replied
with coercion: sharecroppers were beaten, their houses
looted, their cattle impounded; under duress, thousands
signed rent-increase leases. The trouble had begun in 1912,
and the peasants were bitter but powerless. It was this that
made Rajkumar Shukla so resolutely patient in dogging
Gandhi's steps until he brought him to Champaran in 1917.

One day, the Mahatma, in the course of his investiga-
tions, was riding to a village on an elephant, when a
policeman overtook him and drove him back to town.
There Gandhi was served with an official notice to quit
Champaran immediately. He signed the order but wrote
on the back that he would disobey it. He was accordingly
summoned to court the next day.

The area around the courthouse was back with thousands of peasants who had heard that a Mahatma had come
to help them and was in difficulty with the authorities. The
police asked Gandhi to help regulate the crowd. He was
friendly and co-operative; this was concrete proof that their
might, theretofore unquestioned and dreaded, could be
inadequate when challenged.

Inside, Gandhi pleaded guilty. He had disregarded the
order to leave Champaran, he told the court, "not for want
of respect for lawful authority, but in obedience to the
higher law of our being, the voice of conscience." He asked
the penalty due him.

The magistrate said he would announce sentence after
a two-hour recess; until then Gandhi would be released on
bail. Gandhi refused to furnish the bail. He was released

without it. When the court reconvened, the judge declared he would hand down the verdict in several days. Meanwhile he allowed the Mahatma to remain at liberty. Several days later the case was dropped on instructions from above. Civil disobedience had triumphed, Gandhi asserted; the first time in India.

"What I did," Gandhi explained, "was a very ordinary thing. I declared that the British could not order me around in my own country." Not really very ordinary.

Gandhi stayed in Champaran seven months, and returned for two shorter stays. The visit, undertaken casually on the entreaty of an unlettered sharecropper in the expectation that it would last a few days, occupied almost a year of the Mahatma's life. In the end the landlords agreed to forgo further rent increases and refund 25 per cent of the increases already collected. Gandhi felt that the size of the refund was less important than the plantation owners' consent to it.

During his stay in the district, Gandhi brought in a doctor to minister to the peasants and teachers to instruct their children. Kasturbai, too, arrived and taught the women the rules of cleanliness.

The Champaran experience followed a typical Gandhian pattern: it began not as an act of defiance of the British but in an effort to alleviate the misery of the poor. Gandhi's politics grew out of the practical problems of the distressed millions. His was a loyalty not to abstractions but to human beings in their day-to-day living. He did not think out his ideas, he worked them out.

Before leaving Champaran, Gandhi organized a committee of prominent Bihar lawyers, including Rajendra Prasad, later President of free India, to guard the sharecroppers from molestation. The Indian lawyers asked the help of Charles Freer Andrews, an English pacifist missionary who had become the Mahatma's disciple. Andrews agreed but Gandhi objected. "You," he scolded the lawyers, "think that in this unequal fight it would be helpful to have an Englishman on our side. This shows the weakness of your heart. The cause is just and you must rely on yourselves to win the battle."

"He had read our minds correctly," Rajendra Prasad commented, "and we had no reply. . . . Gandhi in this way taught us a lesson in self-reliance."

At the Champaran stage, Gandhi put maximum stress on the regeneration of his own people because he trusted in the British talent for political adaptation. If Indians showed, by their inner discipline, unity, dignity and confidence, that they deserved more freedom, England would grant it. This thesis received a tremendous accession of strength from the adoption, in December, 1916, of the Lucknow Pact between the predominantly Hindu Indian National Congress and the Moslem League, whose president, Mohammed Ali Jinnah, said that his organization now "stands abreast of the Indian National Congress and is ready to participate in any patriotic efforts for the advancement of the country as a whole." With Hindus and Moslems agreed on a broad program of moderate political reform whose presumed benefits both communities would share, many Indians expected early gratification of the Congress petition to "His Majesty the King-Emperor" that "India shall be lifted from the position of dependency to that of an equal partner in the empire along with the self-governing dominions." Their sanguine hope was buoyed by the appointment as Secretary of State for India of Sir Edwin S. Montagu, who, on August 20, 1917, in the House of Commons, did indeed announce a new British policy which envisaged "not only the increasing association of Indians in every branch of the administration" but also the granting of "self-governing institutions with a view to the progressive realisation of responsible government in India as an integral part of the British Empire." These words were taken as a pledge of imminent Dominion status.

Wide circles in Great Britain wanted to satisfy the normal, legitimate political aspirations of India, while others, not so liberal-minded, realized that the war, in which half a million Indian soldiers fought valiantly, and President Woodrow Wilson's doctrine of self-determination, had stirred colonial peoples too deeply to permit a simple return to obtuse antebellum imperialism.

Long ago, the early blood-and-plunder period of Robert Clive, who recorded the "fighting, tricks, chicanery, intrigues, politics, and the Lord knows what" by which England acquired power in India, and of Governor-General Warren Hastings, whose trial in England from February,

1788, to April, 1795, revealed much unscrupulousness and corruption, had come to a close. A year after the 1857 Mutiny the East India Company's rule was abolished, and Queen Victoria, assuming the government of India, appointed Lord Canning her first Viceroy. Thereafter, and slowly, England's ideals of clean government filtered into the administration of India.

Nevertheless, British imperialism could not live down its origins or quiet its fears. "After all," Lord Linlithgow, the British Viceroy, said to me in 1942, "we are the occupying power. Ever since the Mutiny we have hesitated to put arms into the hands of the Indians." From 1858 to 1947, British rule remained a foreign occupation. The British were in India, never of India. Many British officials were devoted to the country, and, after twenty or more years' service, felt at home in India and like foreigners when they went home to England. They ate out their hearts and ruined their health coping with difficult problems and difficult people whose gratitude they craved but rarely received.

The British were masters in somebody else's house. Their very presence was a humiliation. Imperialism is government of other people by other people for other people. It is a perpetual insult, for it assumes that the outsider has the right to rule the insiders who cannot rule themselves. Even if the British had converted India into a land flowing with milk and honey—they did make some deserts flow with ample water—they would have been disliked. Subjection breeds a desire for liberation. Hence imperialism digs its own grave—and there can be no good colonizers.

With the beginning of the twentieth century the number of educated Indians increased. An Indian middle class had arisen; numerous Indians, grown rich in industry and commerce, wanted economic elbow room. Native lovers of power were thwarted by alien rule. Japan's victory over Russia in 1904–5 (the first time a colored Asiatic country had defeated white Europeans) stimulated Indian nationalist opposition to England.

One school of British politicians wished to meet Indian hostility with blood and iron, another to mollify it with reforms. In 1885, Lord Dufferin, the British Viceroy, astutely anticipating popular storms and hoping to channel them into calm legality, sired the Indian National Congress.

Subsequent viceroys blessed it. But the blood-and-iron autocrats did not help the kid-glove moderates.

Torn between their political sagacity and their power lust, the British, through the years, yielded as much of the appearance of power as circumstances required and as little of its substance as conditions permitted. Inevitably, the more concessions they made the more they were asked to make and the die-hards therefore opposed any. To characterize this intransigent mentality, the Hunter Report of 1920, an official British document, quoted General Drake-Brockman of Delhi to the effect that, "Force is the only thing an Asiatic has any respect for." It was a widespread notion in the British administration. So was the concept of Field Marshal Lord Roberts: "It is this consciousness of the inherent superiority of the European which has won us India. However well educated and clever a native may be and however brave he may have proved himself, I believe that no rank which we can bestow on him would cause him to be considered an equal by the British officer."

The Indians knew all this and hated it. Sir Edwin Montagu characterized British rule in India as "far too wooden, far too iron, far too inelastic, and far too ante-diluvian to subserve its purposes in modern times," a composite vegetable-mineral political dinosaur, in other words, incapable of change yet kept alive by feedings at the hands of die-hards in London and blockheads in Delhi. In due course, consequently, Montagu's implied promise of Dominion status, made at the low ebb of Britain's fortunes of war, turned into a yellowing parchment, and when peace came, a disappointed India ran riot.

Gandhi too was disappointed. His mind was a battlefield on which caution constantly contended with passion. Ready to die for a principle, he preferred to compromise and arbitrate. He was a natural fighter and a born peacemaker. He wished to collaborate with the British and hoped that the twentieth century would vanquish the ancient dinosaur. But when Dominion status was shelved, when instead war-time repressive measures were confirmed, the Mahatma took his first deliberate action against British imperialism in India.

## 12  Blood

Secret tribunals had been sentencing people in all parts of India for sedition and opposition. Bal Gangadhar Tilak, foremost Indian nationalist, was imprisoned and so was Mrs. Annie Besant, Irish-born theosophist and brilliant orator who had come to love, live in, and work for India. Two powerful Moslem leaders, the brothers Shaukat and Mohammed Ali, were likewise in jail with thousands of lesser nationalists. Newspapers had been muzzled by wartime censorship.

When the world war ended in November, 1918, Indians expected a restoration of the considerable civil liberties they enjoyed under British rule in normal times. They were painfully surprised when the wartime rigors were continued under the Rowlatt Acts, passed by the New Delhi Imperial Legislative Council on March 18, 1919. Calling this legislation "unjust, subversive of the principle of liberty, and destructive of the elementary rights of the individual on which the safety of the community as a whole and of the state itself is based," Gandhi had campaigned against it. Ineffectiveness riled him. The Mahatma was a symbol of strength to a nation that felt powerless. Despite his frailty he represented virility, he got results, he at least reacted mightily. India had been sapped of her ancient strength, or so Indians thought. Gandhi was restoring her vigor. But all protests against the Rowlatt Acts had been ignored. Indians counted for nothing, Gandhi counted for nothing. What to do?

In Madras recuperating from the effects of dysentery self-induced by dietetic experiments, Gandhi searched for an answer. One morning he announced to his host, Chakravarti Rajagopalachari, later Governor-General of India, "Last night the idea came to me in a dream that we should call on the country to observe a general hartal." A complete suspension of economic activity—shops shut, factories idle, ships unloaded, banks closed—the hartal would bring vast masses into action and demonstrate their unity, discipline, and force.

A hartal lasts a day, two, or three. As a pendant to it,

Gandhi proposed a Satyagraha campaign to begin with prolonged resistance to the Rowlatt Act's limitations on civil
liberties. They planned, as a first step, to sell political literature banned by the government. Gandhi was happy when
six hundred men and women in Bombay signed the Satyagraha pledge. Indians scoffed at the small number. "The
proof of the pudding is in the eating," Gandhi replied. He
had won with fewer in South Africa. "Even such a mighty
government as the Government of India," he declared, "will
have to yield if we are true to our pledge." The pledge, he
emphasized, "is an attempt to introduce the religious spirit
into politics. We may no longer believe in the doctrine of
'tit for tat'; we may not meet hatred with hatred, violence
with violence, evil with evil. . . . Return good for evil."

"Nothing is impossible," he concluded. This keynote
rang with faith in self, people, and God.

The hartal was enormously successful. Gandhi called
it "a most wonderful spectacle." But he did not yet know
his countrymen; he had underestimated their penchant for
violence. In large cities, the hartal was accompanied by
arson, cutting of telegraph wires, plundering of stores,
blocking of trains, and physical assaults on Englishmen. As
penance, Gandhi fasted three days and asked his followers
to fast twenty-four hours. Then he received further news of
violence in small towns. Brusquely, on April 18, 1919, he
called off the entire Satyagraha campaign. It was a "Hima-
layan miscalculation" on his part, he told the country. "I
must now pause and consider how best to meet the situation." He did not worry about losing "face" by admitting
error. He had none of the dictator's yearning for infallibility.
On the contrary, "it is only when one sees one's own mis-
takes with a convex lens, and does just the reverse in the
case of others," he said in his autobiography, "that one is
able to arrive at a just relative estimate of the two." He
exaggerated his own blunders and minimized his neighbor's. Somebody once suggested that he might lose his moral
authority. "Moral authority is never retained by attempting
to hold on to it," was his retort. "It comes without seeking
and is retained without effort." His moral authority resided
in him and ultimately attained an independent existence;
nothing he did, not even the biggest miscalculation or failure, hurt it.

The worst manifestation or post-hartal violence occurred in the Punjab province, notably in Amritsar, a city of 150,000 sacred to the bearded, turbaned, manly-looking Sikhs, and it showed how dangerous were the fires smoldering in British and Indian hearts. Two hartals, on March 30 and April 6, had passed without incident, according to the official British Hunter Commission which investigated the affair: "Europeans could and did walk unmolested amongst the crowds." On August 9, however, the authorities banished from the province two Congress party leaders, a Moslem, Dr. Saifuddin Kitchlew, the same who was received by Stalin just before the dictator's death in March, 1953, and Dr. Satyapal, a Hindu. "Starting in anger at the action of the government in deporting the two local politicians," reads the Hunter Report, a mob raged through the streets. Three prominent Englishmen were killed.

Two days later, Brigadier General Reginald E. H. Dyer a regular British Army officer born in India and an old India hand, took command in Amritsar, and on April 12 issued a proclamation forbidding processions and meetings. But, says the Hunter Report, "it is evident that in many parts of the city the proclamation was not read."

Then the Hunter Report tells the story of the April 13th Jallianwalla Bagh massacre which shaped events in subsequent years and is indelibly written into Indian history. "About one o'clock," the text asserts, "General Dyer heard that the people intended to hold a big meeting about four-thirty P.M. On being asked why he did not take measures to prevent its being held, he replied: 'I went there as soon as I could. I had to think the matter out.'"

"When examined by us," the Hunter Report states, "he [Dyer] explained that his mind was made up as he came along in his motor car; if his orders against holding a meeting were disobeyed he was going to fire at once."

"I had made up my mind," he testified, "I would do all the men to death."

Jallianwalla Bagh, the Report says, "is a rectangular piece of unused ground, covered to some extent by building materials and debris. It is almost entirely surrounded by walls of buildings. The entrances and exits to it are few and imperfect. . . . At the end at which General Dyer entered there is raised ground on each side of the entrance.

A large crowd had gathered at the opposite end of the Bagh and were being addressed by a man on a raised platform about 150 yards from where General Dyer stationed his troops." The Report estimates that there were between ten and twenty thousand people in the Bagh. "None of them were provided with firearms, although some of them may have been carrying sticks," the Report affirms.

Dyer went to the Bagh with twenty-five Gurkha soldiers from Nepal and twenty-five Baluchis from Baluchistan armed with rifles, forty Gurkhas armed only with knives, and two armored cars.

The Hunter Commission's cross-examination of Dyer reads:

"Question: Supposing the passage was sufficient to allow the armored cars to go in, would you have opened fire with the machine guns? Answer: I think, probably, yes."

The armored cars were too big, so, the Report continues, "As soon as General Dyer entered the Bagh, he stationed twenty-five troops on one side of the higher ground at the entrance and twenty-five troops on the other side. Without giving the crowd warning to disperse, which he considered unnecessary as they were in breach of his proclamation, he ordered his troops to fire and the firing continued for about ten minutes.

"As the firing commenced the crowd began to disperse. In all 1,650 rounds were fired. . . . The fire was individual and not volley fire . . . approximately 379 people were killed" and, the Commission estimated, about three times as many wounded. That makes 1,137 wounded, plus 379 dead, or 1,516 casualties for 1,650 bullets. The crowd was a perfect target. The multitude had rushed toward the side of the Bagh with the lowest wall, which was five feet high. Dyer ordered his men to aim at that spot. The Report on Dyer's testimony reads:

"Question: From time to time you changed your firing and directed it to the place where the crowd was thickest? Answer: That is so."

General Dyer's own dispatch to his military superiors, which is quoted in the Hunter Report with his italics, asserts, *It was no longer a question of merely dispersing the crowd, but one of producing a sufficient moral effect not only on those who were present, but more especially* throughout the Punjab. There could be no question of undue severity."

"I thought I would be doing a jolly lot of good," was Dyer's airy summary of the massacre at Jallianwalla Bagh. But the Hunter Commission [whose findings were printed in *East India. Report of the Committee Appointed by the Government of India to Investigate the Disturbances in the Punjab, Etc.* London. His Majesty's Stationery Office, 1920. Cmd 681] decided that, "This was unfortunately a mistaken conception of his duty."

## 13 The Road to Jail

Gandhi answered the Amritsar massacre with a policy: nonco-operation. Boycott British goods, British honors, British courts, British schools, British jobs. He advocated this procedure at a Moslem conference in New Delhi in November, 1919.

In December, 1919, however, the government permitted the annual Congress convention to meet near the site of the massacre and released Shaukat and Mohammed Ali, the two Moslem nationalists, so that they could proceed directly from jail to the session. In the same month, and as further balm for the deep wound inflicted by Dyer, the King-Emperor announced the Montagu-Chelmsford reforms, under which some provincial ministries would be handed over to Indians. "A new era is opening," the monarch proclaimed.

Gandhi hoped so. He asked the Congress session to approve the reforms and help implement them. He abandoned nonco-operation, which he had proposed a month earlier, and counseled co-operation. "To trust is a virtue," he argued. "It is weakness that begets distrust," and he knew Indians did not want to be thought weak.

Gandhi's authority was growing. He was middle class, and the Indian middle class had followed him into politics. Middle-class delegates predominated at the 1919 and subsequent annual Congress meetings. The poor also attended.

Congress, accordingly, adopted a resolution favoring the Montagu-Chelmsford reforms.

But Tilak, Jinnah, and other leading nationalists opposed the reforms (which were a far cry from Dominion status), and postwar disillusionment with British promises was running high. The younger generation had little trust in the British Empire. Lord Chelmsford, the Viceroy, had exonerated Dyer, and the Hunter Report, while condemning the general, recommended no measures against Dyerism. The Moslems were incensed with England for imposing allegedly harsh peace terms on Turkey, an Islamic nation, and deposing the Turkish Sultan-Caliph.

Always eager to unite Hindus and Moslems, always responsive to youth and sensitive to departures from high moral standards, Gandhi returned to his earlier policy of nonco-operation. In December, 1920, the annual Congress convention at Nagpur, reversing its decision of the year before, voted against collaboration with the British. Gandhi thereupon sent his two South African medals to the Viceroy with a letter saying, "I can retain neither respect nor affection for a government which has been moving from wrong to wrong in order to defend its immorality."

This change from love of to rejection of the British Empire—momentous in Gandhi's and India's life—grew out of the Jallianwalla blood bath. The interval of trusting co-operation, reflecting the Mahatma's congenital preference for peaceful accommodation, was quickly closed by country-wide anger. The actions of Gandhi were often shaped by a fear that if he did not lead the people, ugly passions would. His strategy on such occasions was to advance toward the popular goal but insist on his own methods. At the Nagpur Congress session in December, 1920, Gandhi accordingly promised that if India's nonco-operation remained nonviolent, self-government would arrive in a year.

Gandhi carried this message to the people. Motilal Nehru abandoned his lucrative law practice, discontinued the use of alcohol, and became a total nonco-operator. C. R. Das, the leader of the Calcutta bar, Vallabhbhai Patel, a very rich Ahmedabed attorney, Jawaharlal Nehru, and hundreds of others quit the British courts forever. University youth left their classrooms. Teachers and students went into the villages to preach nonco-operation, which, for peasants, meant nonpayment of taxes and nonconsumption of liquors —a double blow at the government's revenue.

For seven months Gandhi toured the countryside in torrid, humid weather, moving in hot, crowded, dirty trains and addressing mass assemblies of a hundred thousand or more, who, in those premicrophone days, could only hope to be reached by his spirit. Clamoring multitudes everywhere demanded a view of the Mahatma; it hallowed them. The inhabitants of one place sent word that if his train did not halt at their tiny station they would lie down on the tracks and be run over by it. The train did stop, and when Gandhi, roused out of a deep sleep, appeared, the crowd, theretofore boisterous, sank to their knees on the railway platform and wept. During those strenuous seven months of travel all his meals, three a day, were the same and consisted of sixteen ounces of goat's milk, three slices of toast, two oranges, and a score of grapes or raisins. They filled him with energy.

Gandhi's long propaganda journey for nonco-operation, on part of which the Moslem Ali brothers accompanied him, had all the attributes of religious revivalism. He told audiences they must not wear foreign clothing, and when they applauded he asked them to strip off all wearing apparel made abroad and pile it in front of him. To this heap of shirts, trousers, coats, caps, shoes, and underwear Gandhi then set a match and as the flames ate their way through the imported goods, he begged everybody to spin and weave their own clothing. He himself took to spinning half an hour per day. He called daily spinning "a sacrament" which turned the spinner's mind "Godward." Soon no Indian came into his presence wearing anything but homespun.

The year passed without the self-government promised by Gandhi. Many nationalists counseled open rebellion against British rule. Dissension in Congress mounted; the Mahatma's emphasis on spinning, temperance, and verbal defiance of the state was ridiculed. Especially the youth demanded action.

"If India takes up the doctrine of the sword," Gandhi replied, "she may gain momentary victory, but then India will cease to be the pride of my heart." His rejection of violence, he said, was adamant "to a point almost bordering on fanaticism," and, since he was now indispensable to the nationalist movement, the Executive Committee of Congress, meeting in Delhi on November 4, 1921, adopted a resolution in favor of a nonviolent, civil-disobedience campaign but simultaneously agreed not to act without his consent. Rabindranath Tagore had reprovingly warned him that the fire that consumed foreign clothing might also inflame minds, and Gandhi was afraid. In December, 1921, and January, 1922, ten thousand Indians were imprisoned for political offenses. Motilal Nehru, C. R. Das, and hundreds of other top Congressmen were already in jail. In several provinces peasants had launched spontaneous nontax movements. India was in an ugly mood.

At the Ahmedabad annual Congress session in December, 1921, Gandhi "in all humility" made one further appeal to Great Britain. "No matter what you do," he exclaimed, "no matter how you repress us, we shall one day wring reluctant repentance from you; and see that you do not make the three hundred millions of Indians your eternal enemies." This challenge to British wisdom was also a plea for help. Gandhi felt apprehensive of what Indians might do under the provocation of repressive measures.

To impress Britain and to satisfy his own and India's need for action, Gandhi now initiated a civil disobedience campaign in the county of Bardoli (population 87,000), near Bombay, where he could personally supervise the experiment. On February 1, 1922, he informed Lord Reading, the new Viceroy, of his plan.

Gandhi restricted civil disobedience to the Bardoli test tube because he was not sure he could keep a nation-wide campaign peaceful and, also, to induce the people of Britain, by a demonstration of Indian restraint, to grant India a fuller measure of independence than they now thought Indians could wisely use.

The Bardoli experiment had hardly commenced when, on February 8, news reached Gandhi of an atrocity committed three days earlier in a small town called Chauri Chaura, in the United Provinces, eight hundred miles from Bardoli. A legal procession took place, "But," as Gandhi reported in *Young India,* "when the procession had passed, the stragglers were interfered with and abused by the constables. The former cried out for help. The mob returned. The constables opened fire. The little ammunition they had was exhausted and they retired to the Thana [city hall] for safety. The mob, my informant tells me, therefore set fire to the Thana. The self-imprisoned constables had to come out for dear life and as they did so they were hacked to pieces and the mangled remains were thrown into the raging flames."

This "brutal murder" of twenty-two policemen was a "bad augury," Gandhi declared. "Suppose," he asked, "the nonviolent disobedience of Bardoli was permitted by God to succeed and the government had abdicated in favor of the victors of Bardoli, who would control the unruly elements that must be expected to perpetrate inhumanity upon due provocation?" He was not sure he could. He accordingly suspended the Bardoli disobedience effort and prohibited any defiance of the government anywhere in India.

"Let the opponent glory in our humiliation or so-called defeat," he cried. "It is better to be charged with cowardice and weakness than to be guilty of denial of our oath and to sin against God. It is a million times better to *appear* untrue before the world than to *be* untrue to ourselves."

At a word from Gandhi, India would have risen in revolt. There were extremists who said that Britain could be driven from the land. The world was still deep in postwar turmoil and England faced difficult crises in many parts of the globe. But Gandhi would not purchase independence at the price of national blood-drenching; a free India born in murder would bear the mark on her forehead for decades. He sacrificed the end, doubtful in any case at that time, because bad means would poison it.

Having canceled civil disobedience, forsworn rebellion, and forbidden open hostility to the state, Gandhi was disarmed, and Lord Reading arrested him.

There had been pressure on Reading from London and by British provincial governors in India to arrest Gandhi, but he resisted it. He had risen from ship's messenger boy to Lord Chief Justice, to Ambassador in Washington, and now Viceroy; his legal mind disapproved of arrest for mere words uttered or written. He declared, "I am quite prepared to face the consequences of Gandhi's arrest if he takes action." Yet when he was sure Gandhi would take no action he ordered his arrest, and for that reason as well as because Gandhi had assured the authorities there would be no consequences. In an article in his weekly, *Young India,* on March 9, 1922, entitled "If I Am Arrested," Gandhi wrote, "Rivers of blood shed by the government cannot frighten me, but I should be deeply pained even if the people did so much as abuse the government for my sake or in my name. It would be disgracing me if the people lost their equilibrium on my arrest." He was arrested on March 10, at 10:30 P.M.

Gandhi had asked for it. The charges were preaching sedition in three published articles. In the first, on September 19, 1921, he said, "I have no hesitation in saying that it is sinful for anyone, either soldier or civilian, to serve this government . . . sedition has become the creed of Congress. . . . Nonco-operation, though a religious and strictly moral movement, deliberately aims at the overthrow of the government and is therefore legally seditious. . . ." In the second, on December 21, 1921, he wrote, "Lord Reading must understand that Nonco-operators are at war with the government. They have declared rebellion against it. . . . Lord Reading is entitled therefore to put them out of harm's way." In the third, on February 23, 1922, Gandhi exclaimed, "How can there be any compromise whilst the British lion continues to shake his gory claws in our face? . . . The rice-eating, puny millions of India seem to have resolved upon achieving their own destiny without further tutelage and without arms. . . . The fight that was commenced in 1920 is a fight to the finish . . ."

The little courtroom in Ahmedabad was crowded on March 18. After the indictment was read and the Advocate-General had stated the case against Gandhi, the Mahatma rose and declared, "I am here . . . to invite and cheerfully submit to the highest penalty that can be inflicted upon me for what in law is a deliberate crime and what appears to me to be the highest duty of a citizen." He then proceeded to explain "why, from a staunch loyalist and co-operator, I have become an uncompromising disaffectionist and non-co-operator." He told of his African experiences, how he had gone to war on the side of the British, and, in India, recruited for their armies. "I was actuated by the belief," he said, "that it was possible by such services to gain a status of full equality in the Empire for my countrymen."

Then, in 1919, came the shocks: The Rowlatt Acts, the Jallianwalla massacre, the floggings, the injustice to the Turkish Caliph. Nevertheless, "I fought for co-operation and working the Montagu-Chelmsford reforms." But "I came reluctantly to the conclusion that the British connection had made India more helpless than she ever was before, politically and economically. . . . She has become so that she has little power of resisting famines. Before the British advent, India spun and wove in her millions of cottages just the supplement she needed for adding to her meagre agricultural resources." The cottage industries had been ruined by British factory products. Though many British officials in India thought they were helping India, "they do not know that a subtle but effective system of terrorism and an organized display of force on the one hand, and the deprivation of all powers of retaliation and self-defense on the other, have emasculated the people and induced in them the habit of simulation." He therefore regarded it "an honor to be disaffected," and requested "the severest penalty."

When Gandhi sat down, Mr. Justice Broomfield bowed to him and pronounced sentence. "The law is no respecter of persons," he stated. "Nevertheless it will be impossible to ignore the fact that you are in a different category from any person I have ever tried or am likely to have to try. It would be impossible to ignore the fact that, in the eyes of millions of your countrymen, you are a great patriot and a great leader. Even those who differ from you in politics look upon you as a man of high ideals and of noble and even saintly life."

So saying, the judge sentenced Gandhi to six years in prison. When the court adjourned most of the spectators fell at Gandhi's feet and wept. Gandhi smiled as he was led away to jail.

This was not the last time the British arrested and imprisoned Gandhi. But it was the last time they tried him.

## 14  Gandhi Fasts

On January 12, 1924, the Mahatma was hastily carried from Yeravda Central Prison to the Sassoon Hospital in the city of Poona, and that evening Colonel Maddock, the British surgeon, operated on him for acute appendicitis. The

operation was successful, and Gandhi thanked the doctor
profusely, but an abscess developed and recovery was slow.
The government thought it generous and wise in these circumstances to release the ailing prisoner and did so on
February 5, 1924. The experience left him with a "very
small . . . capital of energy." In two months, nevertheless,
he was again editing *Young India,* his English-language
weekly, and *Navajivan,* a magazine published in Gujarati,
his native tongue.

During Gandhi's twenty-two months in jail the political
situation in India had deteriorated seriously. Summarizing
it, Gandhi wrote, "Scores of lawyers have resumed practice. Some even regret having given it up. . . . Hundreds of
boys and girls who gave up government schools and col-
leges have repented of their action and returned to them."
A number of nationalist leaders, notably Motilal Nehru, the
father of Jawaharlal, and C. R. Das, had decided to participate in municipal, provincial, and national legislative
bodies in order both to obstruct and instruct the British
authorities. Gandhi disapproved. He remained, he declared
in *Young India* on April 10, 1924, "a strong disbeliever in
this government." But most people were incapable of the
sacrifices nonco-operation demanded, and the Mahatma
saw that the flagging popular temper could not sustain his
anti-Government boycott. He accordingly withdrew from
politics in the usual sense and for the next few years devoted himself to politics in his sense, which was the en-
noblement of the people. "My belief is," he wrote his English friend Charles F. Andrews, "that the instant India is
purified India becomes free, and not a moment earlier."

Purification had no mystic connotation. It meant concrete things like Hindu-Moslem friendship, than which, the
Mahatma asserted, "no question is more important and
more pressing." He agreed with Moslem leader Jinnah that
"Hindu-Moslem unity means Swaraj," home rule. Instead
of unity, however, the two religious communities were at
daggers drawn. "I feel the wave of violence coming," Gandhi announced.

After Gandhi's return to India in 1915, he quickly realized that the relations between Hindus and Moslems would
determine the future of India. He spoke often on the subject and devoted the entire May 29, 1924 issue of *Young*

*India* to his own 6,000-word article on "Hindu-Moslem Tension. Its Cause and Cure." He put the cure in a few words: Hindu-Moslem amity was possible, he said, "because it is so natural, so necessary for both and because I believe in human nature." That sentence contains most of Gandhi. Since the goal is good and man is good, he was saying, the goal can be achieved. Here was the faith that made him the great Mahatma. What did it matter that he failed? He was great even in failure. A person may be smaller in success than in defeat; it depends on what he is trying to do.

In 1946, when India was splitting into Jinnah's Pakistan and Nehru's Indian Republic, to the endless, enormous cost of both, I argued with Mr. Jinnah, who by then had ceased to be the reformer he was in the 1920's, that the world "needs harmony, not new discords," the unification of India, not partition.

"I am a realist," he replied, "I deal with what is."

I called his attention to the mess which religious and nationalistic divisions had made of Europe.

"I must deal with the divisive characteristics which exist," he insisted.

Gandhi too was a realist—"I am a practical realist," he proclaimed—but his was the realism which combats evil instead of using it. Not being a daydreamer, he knew that though man is good the goodness has to be evoked, otherwise somebody would exploit the bad. To evoke the good he fasted for Hindu-Moslem friendship.

Gandhi's fasts were a means of communicating with his fellow men. "Nothing evidently which I say or write can bring the two communities together," he declared; hence the fast. To communicate, the West talks or moves. The East contemplates, sits, suffers. Gandhi availed himself of Western and Eastern methods. When words failed, he fasted.

Throughout life, Gandhi explored new fields of communication. Sometimes he would go to a huge mass meeting, but instead of delivering a speech he would sit cross-legged and sway and say nothing and then he would smile and touch his palms together in the Hindu greeting and the crowd would kneel and weep. He had communicated. He had touched their hearts. In interviews, Gandhi did not merely make statements or answer questions. His chief purpose was to establish a close relationship with the other person because that contributed more to understanding than his words.

A fast, too, was a means of reaching men's hearts and minds. "I fasted," Gandhi once said, "to reform those who loved me," and he added, "You cannot fast against a tyrant," for the tyrant is incapable of love, therefore inaccessible to a weapon of love like fasting. Gandhi never fasted to wring advantages from the British government. His fasts were directed to his own people because between them and him a chord of sympathy presumably existed on which fasting played. A fast had to be unselfish. "I can fast against my father to cure him of a vice," the Mahatma wrote, "but I may not in order to get from him an inheritance." Since a fast was not for personal gain it was for public benefit, and the public would see that and be affected.

Although Gandhi denied it, there was at times an element of intimidation in his fasts as when he fasted because the Ahmedaba millowners, who were devoted to him, refused to accept arbitration in a strike. They submitted lest they kill him; his death from the fast would have been on their hands. But the fast for Hindu-Moslem unity was devoid of compulsion. The Hindu in Allahabad, the Moslem in Agra, would not be compelled to improve relations between the two religions because Gandhi lay dying. They would do so, if at all, when his sacrifice established a kind of common wave-length between him and them. The fast was his way of going out to them and into their hearts so that they could feel what he felt and react as he did. "I am, therefore," he announced, "imposing on myself a twenty-one-day fast from today and ending October 6, 1924. I reserve the liberty," he explained, "to drink water with or without salt." Water during a fast nauseated him and he accordingly would add a pinch of salt or bicarbonate of soda. He drank water because he did not want to die. He loved life and wished to preserve his body. He had it massaged, slept regularly, and walked for strength. All his dietetic aberrations, queer to Westerners and even to many Indians, were designed to make him a biologically perfect instrument for the attainment of spiritual goals, and he remained, until the bullets struck, a stalwart specimen who might have lived years longer. Nevertheless, when moral considerations made a fast imperative, his body had no veto. If the flesh was weak it suffered or even succumbed; it could not say no.

Two Moslem physicians were in constant attendance on Gandhi during the twenty-one-day Moslem-Hindu fast, and Charles Freer Andrews, the Christian missionary, was his nurse. He fasted in the house of Mohammed Ali, the younger brother of Shaukat. For twenty-one days, India's attention would center on that Moslem house. Moslems would see that Mohandas and Mohammed were friends. Hindus would see that their saint had confided his life to a Moslem. Here was a dramatic demonstration of brotherhood.

On the second day of the fast Gandhi wrote a page-long plea for "unity in diversity." "The need of the moment," he asserted, "is not one religion but mutual respect and tolerance of the devotees of different religions." The sixth day he prepared another article on the same theme. The twelfth day he penned one hundred and twelve words for publication which showed how much the emphasis of his politics had shifted. "Hitherto," he affirmed, "it has been a struggle and a yearning for a change of heart among Englishmen who compose the government of India. That change has still to come. But the struggle must for the moment be transferred to a change of heart among the Hindus and the Moslems. Before they dare think of freedom they must be brave enough to love one another, to tolerate one another's religion, even prejudices and superstitions, and to trust one another. This requires faith in oneself. And faith in oneself is faith in God. If we have that faith we shall cease to fear one another." To oppose fear with faith was of Gandhi's essence. The twentieth day he dictated a prayer; the twenty days, he said, had been "days of grace, privilege, and peace."

That evening "Mahatma Gandhi was wonderfully bright and cheerful"; at four A.M. the next day, Andrews reported, "we were called for the morning prayers." He asked Gandhi whether he had slept well. "Yes, very well indeed," Gandhi replied, and, Andrews writes: "It was a happiness to notice at once that his voice was stronger than the morning before . . ."

Six hours later, on the last day of the fast, Gandhi said

to Andrews, "Can you remember the words of my favorite
Christian hymn?"

"Yes, shall I sing it to you now?"

"No, not now," Gandhi explained, "but I have in mind
that when I break my fast we might have a little ceremony
expressing religious unity. I would like the Imam Sahib to
recite the opening verses of the *Koran*. Then I should like
you to sing the Christian hymn, you know the one I mean,
it begins, 'When I survey the wondrous Cross' and ends with
the words, 'Love so amazing, so divine, Demands my soul,
my life, my all.' " This was to be followed by a Hindu
hymn.

At noon, Gandhi spoke in a whisper, asking his many
friends present to "lay down their lives, if need be, for the
cause of brotherhood." The songs were then sung, and
Gandhi drank some orange juice to break the three-week
fast.

There is no evidence that the ordeal was very effective.
Gandhi's love failed to dissolve the granite rock of Hindu-
Moslem hostility which he ascribed, in large measure, to
false notions about the defense of religion. Thus, Hindu
religious processions often passed Mohammedan mosques
at prayer time and that irritated the followers of the Prophet.
It was wrong of Hindus to think their religion required them
to do this and wrong of the Moslems to retaliate with blows.
Equally, Hindus revered the cow and Moslems ate it. But
though Gandhi felt that cow protection symbolized "the
protection of the whole dumb creation of God" and was
therefore "the central fact of Hinduism," he could never
understand, he said, why this aroused so much antipathy
to Moslems. "We say nothing about the slaughter [of cows]
that daily takes place on behalf of Englishmen," he observed. "Our anger becomes red-hot when a Moslem
slaughters a cow." Yet after all, "The cows find their necks
under the butcher's knife because Hindus sell them. . . . In
no part of the world are cattle worse treated than in India.
. . . The half-starved condition of the majority of our cattle
is a disgrace to us."

Music before mosques and cow slaughter did often lead
to Hindu-Moslem riots, but so did the forcible kidnapping
and conversion of women and children from one religious
community by men of the other, or plain rumor as in Bom-

bay in 1938 when a loud quarrel among three Hindus and a Moslem who had been playing cards and drinking in a park started tales of fighting and then actual street battles resulting in a toll of 14 deaths, 98 injured persons, and 2,488 arrests. Such ferocious outbursts stemmed from social and economic circumstances which the Mahatma rarely discussed and usually underestimated. A clue to the situation is to be found in the fact that in the seven hundred thousand villages of India, Hindus and Moslems lived peacefully side by side. In the Indian army, moreover, Hindus, Moslems, Sikhs, and Christians ate, slept, trained and waged war side by side without friction. Hindu-Moslem tensions were an urban, twentieth-century disease, a man-made, middle-class disease which infected some politicians with power madness.

Owing to Islamic precept, the bulk of Moslem wealth in India was invested in land, leaving industry and trade to Hindus and Parsis, who preferred to hire their own co-religionists. The Moslem middle class was therefore late in being born, and when it emerged, early in the century, it could scarcely compete with the Hindus and Parsis who enjoyed advantages of better education and better connections. Young Moslems faced the same stiff competition in obtaining government jobs, which, in view of India's economic backwardness, were a major, if not the major, industry in the country. They consequently insisted that a percentage of those jobs be reserved for them irrespective of their qualifications. Moslem leaders took up this cry, and, of necessity and in fairness, the British yielded.

The Moslems, who constituted one-fourth the population of India, and the Hindus, who comprised three-fourths, are close kin. Most Moslems of India are converted Hindus, converted by the invading Arabs, Afghans, and Persians who began thrusting into India in the eighth century. Mr. Jinnah said converted Hindus constituted 75 per cent of the Moslem population; Pandit Nehru put it at 95 per cent. In parts of India, Moslems worship in Hindu temples. In many areas, Moslems and Hindus are indistinguishable from one another in appearance, dress, language, and custom; Moslems even have castes, like Hindus. Hindi and Urdu, the predominant tongues of Hindus and Moslems, are written with different scripts, and the former has absorbed more Sanskrit words while the latter uses more Persian words, but the two remain very similar. Moreover, in large areas of India, Moslems and Hindus know neither Urdu nor Hindi and have, instead, a common language—Bengali in Bengal, for instance. Jinnah, himself, born in Kathiawar of Hindu ancestry, spoke Gujarati in his father's house, as did Gandhi.

But racial and linguistic ties were sundered by religious differences, and new rivalries for the limited economic opportunities available in India made matters infinitely worse. The Hindu, moreover, is inclined toward separatist isolationism, and of old adopted an attitude of snobbish superiority toward Moslems, refusing, among other things, to intermarry or interdine with them. An orthodox Hindu might visit a Moslem home but would not drink a glass of water or eat there. Moslem politicians, playing on the consequent bitterness, told their followers that independence would mean oppression by the Hindu majority, no jobs in government or business, and perhaps compulsory return to Hinduism. These threats, Jinnah declared in 1917, were unreal. "Fear not," he pleaded, "this is a bogy which is put before you to scare you away from the co-operation and unity which are essential to self-government." Yet the bogy could be made to look so real that in the end he himself used it for its usual purpose.

The British, feeling insecure in India, naturally took advantage of Hindu-Moslem friction. Britain did not *divide* and rule. The Indians were divided. Britain merely divided them a little more in order to rule more easily.

Frustrated by the failure of his Hindu-Moslem fast, Gandhi saw that Dominion status and national freedom were further off than he had thought. In the latter half of 1924, the world subsided into postwar "normalcy." The Dawes Plan undertook to save Germany's economy. The big European powers were recognizing Soviet Russia. Except in South China, where General Chiang Kai-shek had an alliance with Moscow, Bolshevism was in ebb. Coolidge and complacency presided over the United States. The British Empire, jeopardized by the Irish Sinn Fein and Near East revolts between 1919 and 1923, was now becalmed in stagnant waters. In India, the passions of the post-Amritsar period were spent, and doubts and despondency, as well probably as Gandhi's nonviolence, dampened the ardor of belligerent nationalism. This was no time for overt anti-British rebellion. The Mahatma devoted himself to the re-education of a nation for freedom, a slow process.

## 15 Answer to Moscow

Between 1924 and 1929, the doldrum years, Mahatma Gandhi could not have known what the world's newspapers would report in the 1940's and what is now recorded in history. He was merely groping for the road to freedom. Yet the path he trod in that period of India's political depression led to national independence. He would have taken the same course in any case, for what he did in the late 1920's was right in itself, a desirable means no matter what the end. He was convinced that a good means is in itself a good end. This gave him the urge to proceed even though he did not see the light at the exit of the tunnel; it gave him a sense of certainty even though he was not sure of his direction. The use of the proper means, he felt, could never be a loss; it might yield a double gain, there might be benefit from the means plus the attainment of the end. He could therefore be patient, for he was getting somewhere when he did not seem to be moving forward.

Tilak and Gokhale were dead, and the Mahatma had been lifted by the people to the pinnacle of eminence. His hut at Sabarmati ashram was now the White House of India, and on tour hordes besieged him wherever he went. "They will not leave me alone even when I am taking my bath," he wrote. At night his feet and shins were covered with scratches made by men, women, and children who had bowed their heads to the ground and touched him. His deification was commencing; the Gond tribe was worshipping him. "I have expressed my horror and strongest disapproval of this type of idolatry," he cried out.

Many Indians considered him a reincarnation of God, like Buddha and Krishna, God descended temporarily to earth. From the mountains, from the plains, from far-off villages, they came to be sanctified by seeing or touching him. At Dacca, in Bengal, an old man wearing Gandhi's photograph around his neck came forward weeping and said the Mahatma had cured him of chronic paralysis. "You will oblige me by taking that photograph off your neck," Gandhi rebuked him. "It is not I but God who made you whole."

Intellectuals too were not immune. One day a lawyer traveling in the same train with Gandhi fell out, head first. When picked up he was unhurt. The lawyer ascribed his escape to being the Mahatma's fellow traveler. "Then you shouldn't have fallen out at all," Gandhi laughed.

Saddened by the empty glorification, Gandhi wrote, "I am no Mahatma. My Mahatmaship is worthless." He would have preferred Indians to follow in his footsteps rather than kiss his feet. He wanted help, not acclaim and adoration, help, above all, in establishing cottage industries, notably spinning. "For me," he proclaimed, "nothing in the political world is more important than the spinning wheel."

During my stay with Gandhi in 1946, I entered his room while he was spinning. He explained his devotion to it: "If three hundred million people did the same thing once a day not because a Hitler ordered it but because they were inspired by the same ideal, we would have enough unity of purpose to achieve independence." I suggested facetiously that when he stopped spinning to talk to me for an hour he had delayed independence. "Yes," he laughed, "you have postponed Swaraj six yards."

Gandhi's loincloths, shawls, towels, and bedsheets were of homespun, or khadi. More and more Indians were beginning to wear it. But some sneered at it. "Monotonous white shrouds," they mocked. "The livery of our freedom," Jawaharlal Nehru replied.

Gandhi believed so much in the spinning wheel that he put it in the center of the flag of the Congress party, which became the flag of independent India. It was his peculiar contribution to the education of the politically minded in the cities; he made them conscious of the poor, uneducated peasantry. It was an adventure in identification between leadership and masses, for he knew how easily in India the gold-silver-silk-jewel-elephant splendor of her palaces or, in more modern terms, the glamor of giant industrial units, might hide from view the animal poverty in her hovels.

To assist the underdog, Gandhi taught, you must understand him, and to understand him you must sometimes live as he does and work as he does. "I am trying to work from the bottom upward," he declared, and he warned intellectuals that if they did not support his khadi policy "educated India will cut itself off from the only visible and tangible tie that binds them to the masses." Spinning was thus another channel of communication, and a labor of love.

To organize and finance the spinning-wheel movement was the chief purpose of several of his country-wide tours. Usually he traveled third class. He suggested that if the Viceroy, the Commander-in-Chief, and the maharajas did likewise, third-class hygienic conditions would be improved. Wherever he went he collected money. All through life he was an irrepressible fund raiser. The sums were used to buy spinning wheels for peasants, open city stores for village khadi, and train spinning and weaving teachers. As his train stopped at stations he would cup his palm out the window so people could put coins and bills into it. Or he would pass among the crowd selling homespun. He also accepted gold and jewels. "The army of my sweethearts is daily increasing," he boasted. "The latest recruit is Ranibala of Burdwan, a darling perhaps ten years old. I dare not ask her age. I was playing with her as usual and casting furtive glances at her six heavy gold bangles. I gently explained to her that they were too heavy a burden for her delicate little wrists and down went her hand on the bangles." Later that day he reported this success to a women's meeting and got "quite a dozen bangles and two or three pairs of earrings, all unasked. Needless to say, they will be used for khadi." He explained to the women that they would improve their beauty by giving him the ornaments: "Handsome is as handsome does," he quoted. Besides, he said, Indian women wore too much "personal furniture" on their ears, noses, arms, and ankles. They would be cleaner without it.

Friends accused him of exaggerating the efficacy of spinning. This was the machine age, they claimed, and all his work, wisdom, and holiness would not turn back the clock. "A hundred and fifty years ago," Gandhi replied, "we manufactured all our cloth. Our women spun fine yarns in their own cottages, and supplemented the earnings of their husbands. . . . India requires nearly thirteen yards of cloth per head per year. She produces, I believe, less than half the amount. India grows all the cotton she needs. She ex-

ports several million bales of cotton to Japan and Lancashire and receives much of it back in manufactured cálico,
though she is capable of producing all the cloth and all the
yarn necessary for supplying her wants by hand-weaving
and hand-spinning. . . . The spinning wheel was presented
to the nation for giving occupation to the millions who had,
at least four months of the year, nothing to do."

Gandhi's paramount compulsion was to help the under-
employed poor, and since he and his God were partners,
he enlisted the Almighty in his tasks. "To a people famish-
ing and idle," he wrote, "the only acceptable form in which
God can dare appear is work and promise of food as
wages." Poverty, he held, led to "moral degradation." He
wanted a prosperous and happy India. "If we do not waste
our wealth and energy," he urged, "the climate and natural
resources of our country are such that we can become the
happiest people in the world."

The rather widespread notion that Gandhi favored poverty is due, probably, to the fact that he took it upon himself voluntarily and decried extremes of wealth. "In South
Africa, where I had the privilege of associating with thousands of our countrymen on most intimate terms," he once
declared, "I observed almost invariably that the greater the
possession of riches, the greater was their moral turpitude."
Then he quoted Jesus, "It is easier for a camel to go through
the eye of a needle than for a rich man to enter the Kingdom
of God." He told the rich to make themselves poorer by
giving to the poor.

In Bengal, Gandhi was the guest of a landlord who served
him milk in a gold bowl and fruit on gold plates. "Where
did he get these plates from?" Gandhi later asked. "From
the substance of the peasants," he answered. "Where their
life is one long-drawn-out agony, how dare he have these
luxuries?"

Gandhi feared that industrialization would throw peasants and workingmen out of work and increase India's
"grinding pauperism." He accordingly preferred cottage
spinning to textile mills. "If you multiply individual production to millions of times," he contended, "would it not
give you mass-production on a tremendous scale? But I
understand that your 'mass-production' is a technical term
for production by the fewest possible number through the

aid of highly complicated machinery. I have said to myself that that is wrong. My machinery must be of the elementary type which I can put into the homes of the millions." His slogan was "a miniature mill in every home."

"So," an interviewer summed up in November, 1934, "you are opposed to machinery only because and when it concentrates production and distribution in the hands of the few?"

"You are right," Gandhi replied. "I hate privilege and monopoly. Whatever cannot be shared with the masses is taboo to me. That is all."

It is interesting that today in India, where much of Gandhi's teaching is ignored, his economics, once considered retrograde or naïve, are being accepted by a growing body of Westernized, modern-minded Indians, by the Socialists, for instance, and by some members of the government. Industries are of course necessary, but in many Asian and African countries they bring prolonged mass unemployment and misery rather than mass prosperity and useful leisure. Persons displaced by a complex lathe are not soon absorbed into other jobs; they starve. "If industries in India are completely mechanized it would not be possible to give employment to all our people," the Prime Minister of Bombay state said in December, 1952.

In the streets of Madras, under the broiling August sun, I have seen chocolate-skinned men, wearing only turbans and loincloths, pulling and pushing heavy loads on wheeled platforms the size of two-ton trucks. Their labor is cheaper than that of animals. They would resent the employment of oxen or horses, not to speak of an automotive vehicle. Gandhi was not anti-West or anti-industry; his Indian eye simply saw the economic problems of India and Asia more clearly than the blind Europeanized votaries of machines for machines' sake.

Challenged to boredom as to whether he objected to machinery, Gandhi exclaimed, "How can I when I know that even this body is a most delicate piece of machinery? The spinning wheel is a machine; a little toothpick is a machine. What I object to is the craze for machinery, not machinery as such. Today," he continued, "machinery merely helps a few to ride on the backs of the millions. The machine should not tend to atrophy the limbs of man. For instance, I would make intelligent exceptions. Take the case of the Singer sewing machine. It is one of the few useful things ever invented, and there is a romance about the device itself." He had learned to sew on it. And would you not need big factories to produce such devices?

"Yes," he agreed. "Ideally," he added in a typically Gandhian circular argument, "I would rule out all machinery, even as I would reject this very body, which is not helpful to salvation, and seek absolute liberation of the soul. From that point of view I would reject all machinery, but machines would remain because, like this body, they are inevitable." In the same mood he said, "It is and it is not," when two American women asked whether it is true that he objected to railways and other means of speedy locomotion.

Nor did Gandhi reject Western amenities and skills. "The West," he wrote Miss Madeline Slade, "has always commanded my admiration for its surgical inventions and all-round progress in that direction." But being very Indian, and disinclined to imitate the West slavishly or to try to impress anybody with an advanced technological superstructure built on the rotten base of mass backwardness, Gandhi would have concentrated first on the Indian village where, by the admission of all authorities, machine-minded Americans included, overpopulation makes almost all machines superfluous.

From time immemorial, India's chief defense against the invader was her villages. Invaded twenty-six times and always from the West, India fears the West and enjoys defying and condemning it. Gandhi's maximum confidence in his country made him the least of its isolationists and he wanted "the cultures of all lands to be blown about my house as freely as possible" (though he refused to "be blown off my feet by any"), but for an emergency the central redoubt, the last fortress, against the armed or unarmed intruder would be the peasantry. Foreigners might conquer and rule in federal and provincial capitals and even in districts, but the villages, singly unimportant and remote, had their own inner Gibraltar—a cohesive, popular, internal organization which Gandhi wished to keep intact. He spoke frequently of the Panchayat or Council of Five Elders, who from ancient days governed each village autonomously, and he also advocated economic independence for the village. His ideal village, he wrote in *Harijan* of July 26, 1942, would be a "complete republic, independent of its neighbors for its vital wants, and yet interdependent for many wants in which dependence is a necessity." It would feed itself and grow "useful crops"—not opium—for sale, and have schools, a theater, a clean water supply, public halls, and electricity in every hut—surely evidence of his acceptance of western techniques when they benefit the mass of needy individuals.

A self-governing, self-reliant village, trading chiefly with nearby self-sufficient villages and importing a minimum of complicated appliances, was Gandhi's recipe for democracy in Asia. The more these small geographic units achieved by co-operative effort at the bottom the less room there would be for dictatorship from above and afar. He preferred them to the hot, dirty, herring-barrel cities of India with their factory slums.

There is no support for the oft-repeated assumption that Mahatma Gandhi advocated regress to a preindustrial society; he wanted progress with the aid of western technology but not at the expense of man the animal and man the spiritual human being. The evils of European industrialism. compounded by eastern exploitation, are not a pretty sight in India and elsewhere in Asia.

On a higher, philosophical level, Gandhi simply realized, earlier than most, the dangers and horrors of a civilization in which machinery may enslave man instead of performing its essential function of liberating him. In London, in 1931, Charlie Chaplin asked to see Gandhi. Gandhi, who had never seen a moving picture film, did not know the name, and on being enlightened said he had no interest in actors. But when told the actor came from a poor family in the slums of Lambeth, London, he received him. The conversation started, as it often did in the case of Westerners, with the visitor's misconception about Gandhi's attitude to machinery, and the answer apparently so impressed Chaplin that he devoted one of his pictures to the daily race between men and machines.

The faster machines move the faster man lives and the bigger the tribute in nervous tension he pays to the machine. Culture, leisure, indeed living, become so interlinked with machines that man himself may be innerly impoverished.

The individual is somewhat in the position of the savage who makes an idol and then serves it. To Gandhi, mechanization or any other form of progress was not an end in itself; he judged material advances by their moral and spiritual effect on human beings. The individual was his central concern. And he judged individuals not by what they had but by what they were, not by property but personality, not by outer fortune but inner riches. His was the individualism of worth, not of wealth. Industrialization made men rich, but did it make them men? As the greatest individual of the twentieth century, if not of twenty centuries, certainly the most fervent defender of individualism in our era, Gandhi wondered how much rugged materialism could contribute to the stature of individuals. He dreamt of a prosperous India which, however, did not feed its people into a machine that cut them down to standardized, conforming pygmies. Observing the world, he identified industrialization with materialism and feared both as menaces to man's growth. His belief in and defense of the individual naturally made him anti-Communist, yet he saw Communism as the end product of a process which corrodes non-Communist countries too, and the attitude, therefore, which made him an opponent of the Soviet system also induced him to criticize Western civilization; between the two he saw a difference of degree rather than of kind. "Bolshevism," Gandhi affirmed, "is the necessary result of modern materialistic civilization. Its insensate worship of matter has given rise to a school which has been brought up to look upon materialistic advancement as the goal of life and which has lost touch with the final things in life. . . . I prophesy that if we disobey the law of the final supremacy of spirit over matter, of liberty and love over brute force, in a few years' time we shall have Bolshevism rampant in this land which was once so holy." This referred to India but might have been said of any country. The West, perhaps, is so frightened of Bolshevism, or Stalinism, or Sovietism, because it feels the germ of the same disease within itself.

Gandhi had the answer and antidote to Stalinism: a big, brave, spirit-over-matter individual who could resist invasions of his freedom because he put principles above possessions. This prescription would defeat Communism and cure democracy.

In all Gandhi's speeches, writings, fasts, political acts, in all his struggles with Marshal Smuts in South Africa and with the British and his own people in India, he was coping with the one issue which confronts every person on the planet: How can the modern individual maintain his inner peace and outer security, how can he remain honest, free, and himself in the face of the assaults being made upon him by the power of mighty governments, the power of mighty economic organizations, the power of evil that resides in cruel majorities and militant minorities, and the power now extractable from the atom? Most people stand in awe of these agglomerations of power, admit their inability to fight them, and submit. The result, in all countries, is a shrinking man. This opens the door to totalitarianism and threatens democracy, for without an individual who is ready and able to defend himself against the inroads of power, freedom is doomed.

Power was the chief preoccupation of Lenin and Stalin. Distrusting the individual, who must therefore be watched and crushed, they founded a movement and state on the leadership principle: an "elite" party, dominated by one man, leads the obedient "masses." Hence the dehumanized dictatorship. Gandhi's chief preoccupation was with the individual, whom he trained in assertion of self and will not only against the British state but against any state. "Gandhi has straightened our back and stiffened our spines," Nehru said. Power cannot ride on an upright back.

The individual's strength of spirit must at least keep pace with the expansion of bureaucratic, economic, and scientific power, otherwise he will be beaten into a robot slave. On the outcome of the race between man and power depends the future of modern civilization.

Gandhi devoted much of his life to studies in nutrition; he sought vitamins for the body and foods that make men big. His menu for the growth of individuals was fearlessness. Prophet of nonviolence, he nevertheless declared that "where there is a choice between cowardice and violence, I would choose violence," for cowardice reduces a man's self-respect and hence his stature. Gandhi himself had no fear; it is this more than any other quality which accounts for his growth from the ordinary person he was in his twenties and early thirties to the mountain of a man he ul-

timately became. He did not fear governments, jails, death
—it would unite him with his God— illness—he could
conquer it— hunger, unpopularity, criticism, or rejection.

Gandhi's individualism fed on courage. Nonviolence, he
said, requires much more courage than violence. No coward
would sit still on the ground as galloping police horses advanced upon him or lie in the path of an automobile or
stand without moving as baton-swinging policemen laid
about them. This was active resistance of the brave. Gandhi
applied a technique of combat which turned the traditional docility of the gentle Hindu into heroism. The method
stemmed from his faith in common clay. He equated the last
with himself and himself with the last. "The ideals that
regulate my life," he wrote, "are presented for the acceptance of mankind in general. . . . I have not the shadow of
a doubt that any man or woman can achieve what I have
if he or she would make the same effort and cultivate the
same hope and faith. I am but a poor struggling soul yearning to be wholly good. . . . I know that I have still before
me a difficult path to traverse." He recognized human weaknesses in himself and others and did not expect perfection
in anybody, but he did believe in the individual's corrigi-
bility and endless capacity to climb. Refusing to concentrate
on the bad in people, he often changed them by regarding
them not as what they were but as though they were what
they wished to be, as though the good in them was all of
them. Such creative optimism sometimes added inches or
cubits to the heights of his associates, and even the casual
visitor felt its potential benefits.

A perpetual reformer of men, Gandhi nevertheless accepted them as they were. Love made him indulgent. He
had an extremely strict code of conduct for himself and a
lenient one for others. He lived in happy harmony with men
and women invited by him to the ashram who did not believe in God, or in nonviolence, or in chastity, or in him.
In fact, he encouraged rebellion and nonconformity as aids
in the development of the individual. Disloyalty to him
never disturbed him, disloyalty to principle did.

The universal disloyalty to principle under all social sys-
tems is due to its cost. Under dictatorship the price may be
death, in a democracy discomfort and embarrassment.
Gandhi was ready to pay no matter what the cost. The

poorer he was in material things the more he could pay, and the richer it left him in the coin of the spirit, which was the only currency he valued.

He nourished the same attitude in others. He told his associates to sacrifice their relationship and contacts with him for the sake of their beliefs. He was not merely leading a movement and striving for its success, he was forging a nation by molding men. If he was to be the father of a nation, he wanted giant sons. When faced with opposition in the Congress party or in his immediate ashram entourage he sometimes yielded to it when he could easily have broken it; he respected dissent. It is the hallmark of manhood. At a conference, once, on basic education, all participants agreed with Gandhi except Zakir Hussain, a Moslem schoolmaster. Gandhi appointed him president of the society for basic education. The Mahatma's own strength of will and fanatic faith in principles might have made him a dictator—he had a streak of the dictator in him—but his interest in the growth of individuals made him a democrat.

Gandhi's following, consequently, became large, diverse, and diffuse. He also attracted a wide assortment of leaders. Pyarelal Nayyar, for many years Gandhi's chief secretary, enumerated some of them in the *Harijan* magazine of March 15, 1952. The Mahatma's "intimate circle," he wrote, "included shrewd capitalists and business men like G. D. Birla and Seth Jamnalal Bajaj, sceptics like Acharya Kripalani and intellectuals and revolutionaries like Pandit Jawaharlal Nehru, statesmen and astute politicians like Pandit Motilal Nehru and Vithalbhai Patel, men of faith and renunciation like Vinoba Bhave, subtle-minded lawyers like Rajagopalachari, humanitarians like Dr. Rajendra Prasad, profound scholars and divines like Maulana Azad, brilliant medicoes —geniuses in their own line—like the late Dr. Ansari and Hakim Ajmal Khan Saheb, colorful personalities like the irreverent, motherly nightingale of India—Sarojini Naidu; blue-blooded society ladies like Miss Slade; and last but not least our Man of Iron, the granite pillar of free India— alas, now fallen—Sardar Patel. This list is only illustrative."

"What," asks Pyarelal, "was the secret of his amazing hold over the minds and loyalties of men?" His "intense and many-sided realism," he replies; "his tact; deep sympathy";

"his delicacy and personal charm. . . ." The capitalists were drawn to him "by his shrewdness in practical affairs, sincerity and courage; Acharya Kripalani became his bond-slave when he found him the rebel and revolutionary that he himself aspired to be; Pandit Jawaharlal Nehru—refined and intellectual—was captured by his dynamism and artistry of life. I remember how, on one occasion in the course of a heated discussion, Nehru impatiently broke out, 'I want revolution, this is reformism,' to which Gandhiji rejoined, 'I have made revolutions while others have talked about them. When your exuberance has subsided and your lungs are exhausted, you will come to me, if you are really serious about making a revolution.' "

Motilal Nehru, the father of Jawaharlal, likewise had his differences with Gandhi. "I have told Mahatmaji," the elder Nehru once reported to Pyarelal, " 'I do not believe in your spirituality and am not going to believe in God at least in this life.' "

"And what did he say in reply?" Pyarelal gasped.

"He only laughed," said Motilal Nehru.

Maulana Azad, the Islamic scholar, Pyarelal continues, "found in him a divine to match and a religious catholicity in action"; Vinoba regarded Gandhi as a saint of ancient India; "Rajagopalachari found in him a clarity of thinking and perspicacity, a marvellous, quick grasp of his opponent's case and a legal acumen which put to shame the forensic acrobatics of the conventional legal celebrities." The doctors welcomed his interest in health; Mrs. Naidu discovered that he was "a poet in action." Madeline Slade, daughter of a knighted British admiral, Pyarelal remarks, received from him "that deep spirituality which the starved soul of the Mammon-worshipping West hungered for," and Sardar Vallabhbhai Patel, the statesman-machine-boss, master of the Congress party, "found that in Gandhiji at last there was a political leader who was no talker, but a man of action who made things happen and who never failed to deliver the goods once he had undertaken to do so."

Grant that these are the encomiums of a faithful disciple, they nevertheless approximate the truth, for Gandhi did actually attract and lead these big men and women and many others. He had power over them, Pyarelal explains, because "Gandhiji never put anybody to a use which was not in the best interests of the person concerned. He so used his instruments as to draw out and develop the best in them so that they grew in strength and stature from day to day. . . . In argument he never tried to overbear or overwhelm the opponent by intellectual bludgeoning. He made the opponent a fellow seeker after truth. The aim always was to convert, never to coerce or suppress. The opponent never smarted under the humiliation of defeat but shared in full the thrill and joy of the discovery of truth which he was made to feel was as much his as Gandhiji's. This made the mind of the opponent receptive, instead of being resistant." Hence Gandhi's boast, "I am a born democrat."

Mahatma Gandhi loved not mankind in the abstract but men, women, and children, and he hoped to help them as specific individuals and groups of individuals. He belonged to them and they knew it and therefore they belonged to him. By harboring the disloyal, he dispelled their disloyalty. His loyalty begot theirs. In this wise, during the worst years of defeat and depression from 1924 to 1929, he prepared for later triumphs. India now called him "Bapu," Father.

## 16 The Salt of Freedom

In 1928, India seethed with labor and nationalist unrest. In December of that year, Assistant Police Superintendent Saunders of Lahore was assassinated. Gandhi branded it "a dastardly act." Bhagat Singh, the presumed killer, eluded arrest and quickly achieved the status of hero. On April 8, 1929, he walked into the Legislative Assembly in New Delhi while the chamber was filled with its British and Indian members, tossed two bombs into their midst and then began firing from a pistol. Fortunately only one legislator was seriously hurt.

In the province of Bengal, always the hearth of turbulence and of opposition to the British as well as to the Congress leadership, Subhas Chandra Bose, a stormy petrel whose slogan was, "Give me blood and I promise you freedom," had recruited a big, restive following. Jawaharlal Nehru's Independence-Now oratory won him popularity with the youth.

A battle impended, but Gandhi moved into it cautiously. It had to be a battle in which his side would fight with a special kind of weapon: civil disobedience. No government arsenal produced it. Unlike most rebels, Gandhi did not get ammunition from his adversary.

En route to the annual Congress session in Calcutta in December, 1928, friends questioned Gandhi when his train stopped at Nagpur. "What would be your attitude toward a political war of independence?" they asked.

"I would decline to take part in it," he answered. "Today I am teaching the people how to meet a national crisis by nonviolent means."

But at the session, the young men led by Bose and Nehru demanded action. They advocated a declaration of independence and, by implication, a war of independence. Gandhi urged a two-year warning to the British. Under pressure, he cut it down to one year. If by December 31, 1929, freedom had not been achieved under Dominion status, Gandhi announced, "I must declare myself an Independence-Walla. . . . I have burnt my boats." The showdown would come in 1930.

Lord Irwin, later Lord Halifax, the Viceroy, according to Alan Campbell Johnson, his biographer, "was largely absorbed," during the first four months of 1929, "with finding administrative remedies to meet the perils of political terrorism and industrial strife." Labor and trade union officials were arrested by the score. The remedy of course lay not in these measures but in statesmanship. This loomed as a possibility when the British Labour party took office in England with Ramsay MacDonald, a champion of Indian freedom, as Prime Minister. Gandhi felt encouraged. In *Young India* magazine of May 9, 1929, he uttered the hope that freedom would come nonviolently "through a gentlemanly agreement with Great Britain. But then," he cautioned, "it will not be an imperialistic haughty British maneuvering for world supremacy but a Britain humbly trying to serve the common end of humanity." In the summer Lord Irwin went to London, spent several months in conferences with the new government, and returned to Delhi to announce on October 31, 1929, that His Majesty's Government envisaged a Round Table Conference of British and Indian delegates; he stated moreover that "the natural issue of India's constitutional progress . . . is the attainment of Dominion status."

Gandhi and the older nationalist leaders responded favorably to this prospect and, undeterred by protests from Jawaharlal Nehru and Subhas Chandra Bose and their clamant supporters, prepared to compromise. An interview with Lord Irwin was arranged for the afternoon of December 23. In London meanwhile, Lord Reading, the former Viceroy, led an attack on MacDonald's India policy in the House of Lords, and in the House of Commons, the Tories and Liberals combined against the Labour government, which commanded only a parliamentary minority, to condemn Irwin's premature pledge of Dominion status. The afternoon interview with Gandhi, Jinnah, Motilal Nehru, Vitalbhai Patel, and Sir Tej Bahadur Sapru, a great constitutional lawyer, accordingly ended in the Viceroy's declaring "that he was unable to prejudge or commit the [Round Table] Conference at all to any particular line. . . ."

This was the disturbing overture to the notable annual Congress session in Lahore in December, 1929, under the presidency of Jawaharlal Nehru, who had celebrated his fortieth birthday the month before. With Gandhi as stage director, the session unfurled the flag of freedom and adopted a resolution for unabridged independence and secession from the Empire. "Swaraj is now to mean complete independence," Gandhi asserted. The Congress instructed its members and friends to withdraw from the legislatures, and sanctioned civil disobedience and nonpayment of taxes. The Congress executive committee was authorized to decide when the Satyagraha campaign would commence but, as Gandhi said, "I know that it is a duty devolving primarily on me." He would have to be the heart, brain, and directing hand of any civil disobedience movement, and he, therefore, would choose the hour, place, and precise issue. He withdrew to his ashram to contemplate.

The country was tense with suspense. Rabindranath Tagore, for whom Gandhi had the deepest veneration, was in the neighborhood of Sabarmati Ashram and came for a visit on January 18. Piqued by curiosity, he inquired what the Mahatma had in store for India in 1930. "I am furiously thinking day and night," Gandhi replied, "and I do not see any light coming out of the surrounding darkness."

"There is a lot of violence in the air," Gandhi stated. In these circumstances civil disobedience, the only alternative to "armed rebellion," involved "undoubted risks," and he was therefore searching for a form of civil disobedience which could not explode into nation-wide violence. For six weeks he searched while the country waited impatiently. India's eyes were on Gandhi's hut.

Presently he knew what he would do.

Before proceeding with his plan he communicated it to the Viceroy, for he always held that "any secrecy hinders the real spirit of democracy." The letter to Irwin was surely the strangest ever received by the head of a government. "Dear Friend," it began. "Before embarking on Civil Disobedience and taking the risk I have dreaded to take all these years, I would fain approach you and find a way out." He believed in negotiation which might give the adversary an alternative. "I cannot intentionally hurt anything that lives, much less human beings, even though they may do the greatest wrong to me and mine," the letter continued. "Whilst, therefore, I hold the British rule to be a curse, I do not intend harm to a single Englishman or to any legitimate interest he may have in India. . . . And why do I regard the British rule as a curse? It has impoverished the dumb millions by a system of progressive exploitation and by a ruinous expensive military and civil administration which the country can never afford. It has reduced us politically to serfdom. It has sapped the foundations of our culture. . . . I fear . . . there has never been any intention of granting . . . Dominion status to India in the immediate future. . . ."

Then Gandhi particularized. In an independent India, he wrote, the whole revenue system would have to be "revised so as to make the peasant's good its primary concern. But the British system seems to be designed to crush the very life out of him. Even the salt he must use to live is so taxed as to make the burden fall heaviest on him. . . . The tax shows itself still more burdensome on the poor man when it is remembered that salt is the one thing he must eat more than the rich man." Elsewhere he explained that the peasant's salt tax amounted to three days' income a year. The peasant used more salt than the rich because he perspired more while working in the fields under the scorching tropical sun of India. Gandhi's letter complained further that "The drink and drug revenue, too, is derived from the poor. It saps the foundations both of their health and morals.

"The iniquities sampled above," the Mahatma charged, "are being maintained in order to carry on a foreign administration demonstrably the most expensive in the world. Take your own salary," he said to the Viceroy. "It is over 21,000 rupees [about $7,000] a month, besides many other indirect additions. . . . You are getting over 700 rupees a day [approximately $233] against India's average income of less than two annas [four cents] a day. Thus you are getting much over five thousand times India's average income. The British Prime Minister is getting only ninety times Britain's average income. On bended knee I ask you to ponder this phenomenon. I have taken a personal illustration to drive home a painful truth. I have too great a regard for you as a man to wish to hurt your feelings. I know that you do not need the salary you get. Probably the whole of your salary goes to charity. But a system that provides such an arrangement deserves to be summarily scrapped. What is true of the Viceregal salary is true generally of the whole administration. . . .

"Nothing but organized nonviolence," Gandhi wrote further, "can check the organized violence of the British government. . . . This nonviolence will be expressed through civil disobedience. . . . My ambition is no less than to convert the British people through nonviolence, and thus make them see the wrong they have done to India."

Then he pleaded for negotiations. "I respectfully invite you to pave the way for the immediate removal of these evils, and thus open a way for a real conference between equals."

"But"—and this was Gandhi's plan—"if you cannot see your way to deal with these evils and if my letter makes no appeal to your heart, on the eleventh day of this month I shall proceed with such co-workers of the Ashram as I can take, to disregard the provisions of the Salt Laws. . . . It is, I know, open to you to frustrate my design by arresting me. I hope that there will be tens of thousands ready, in a disciplined manner, to take up the work after me."

Lord Irwin did not reply; his secretary sent an acknowledgment. He refused to see Gandhi, nor did he arrest him.

As March 11th neared, India bubbled with excitement. Scores of foreign and domestic newspapermen dogged Gandhi's footsteps in the ashram; what exactly would he do? Thousands camped around the village to witness the spectacle. Cables from the world kept the Ahmedabad post office humming. "God guard you," the Reverend Dr. John Haynes Holmes telegraphed from New York.

On March 12, prayers having been sung, the Mahatma and seventy-eight male members of the ashram, whose names and personal particulars were published in *Young India* for the convenience of the police, left the village on foot. "We are marching in the name of God," Gandhi said.

They headed due south toward the sea. For twenty-four days they walked. Gandhi leaned on a lacquered bamboo staff an inch thick and 54 inches long with an iron tip. A horse was available for Gandhi but he never used it. "Less than twelve miles a day in two stages with not much luggage! Child's play!" he declared. Some days they did fifteen miles. He was sixty-one. Several ashramites became fatigued and footsore. "The modern generation is delicate, weak and much pampered," he commented. He spun an hour every day and kept a diary.

Gandhi and his moving congregation followed winding dirt roads from village to village. Peasants sprinkled the roads and strewed leaves on them. Every settlement on the line of march was festooned with the national colors. As the pilgrims passed, peasants who had gathered from the countryside sank to their knees. Two or three times a day the marchers halted for meetings where the Mahatma and others exhorted the population to wear and make homespun, abjure alcohol and opium, abandon child marriage, and live pure lives.

In the area traversed, over three hundred village headmen gave up their government jobs. The inhabitants of a village would usually accompany the marchers to the next, as a sort of honor guard. From all over India young men and women arrived to attach themselves to the advancing column of ashramites. When Gandhi reached the sea at Dandi on April 5th, his small band had grown into a nonviolent army several thousand strong.

The entire night of April 5th, the ashramites did not sleep but prayed, and early in the morning they accompanied the Mahatma to the sea. He dipped into the water, returned to the beach, and there picked up some salt left by the waves. Mrs. Sarojini Naidu, standing by his side, cried, "Hail, Deliverer."

Gandhi thus broke the British law which made it a punishable crime to possess salt not purchased from the government salt monopoly. He himself had not used salt for six years.

Had Gandhi gone by train or automobile to make salt, the effect would have been considerable. But to walk two hundred and forty-one miles in twenty-four days and rivet the attention of all India, to trek across the countryside saying, "Watch, I will give a signal to the nation," and then to pick up a palmful of salt in publicized defiance of a mighty government, that required imagination, dignity, and the sense of showmanship of a great artist. It appealed to illiterate peasants and it fascinated sophisticated critics like Subhas Chandra Bose who compared the Salt March to "Napoleon's march to Paris after his return from Elba."

The act performed, Gandhi withdrew from the scene. India had its cue; he had communicated with it by stealing some salt from a beach.

Along India's long seacoast and in her numerous bays and inlets, peasants waded into the water with pans and produced salt illegally. The police made mass arrests. Congress volunteers sold contraband salt in the cities. Many received short prison terms. The police raided the Congress party headquarters in Bombay where salt was being made in pans on the roof. A protesting crowd of sixty thousand assembled; hundreds were handcuffed or their arms fastened with ropes and led off to jail. The salt lifted by Gandhi from the beach at Dandi was sold to the highest bidder for 1600 rupees, over $500, which went to a public fund. Jawaharlal Nehru was sentenced to six months for infringing the Salt Act. The Mayor of Calcutta received a similar sentence for reading seditious literature to a public meeting and urging a boycott of foreign textiles. Kishorlal Mashruwala, one of the Mahatma's most faithful disciples, was incarcerated for two years. Many towns observed hartals when Congress leaders were arrested.

Whole provinces were deprived of their nationalist leaders. Vithalbhai Patel, the speaker of the federal Legislative Assembly, resigned and advised Indians to boycott the government. At Peshawar, on the northwest frontier, the police and military were driven from the city; subsequently, troops retook the town and killed seventy and wounded one hundred. The government placed all nationalist newspapers under censorship. The Viceroy, writes Lord Irwin's biographer, "had filled the jails with no less than sixty thousand political offenders." A month after Gandhi had bathed in the sea at Dandi, India seethed in angry yet peaceful revolt. Eager to continue the movement and knowing, from experience, that Gandhi would cancel it if they were violent, Indians remained nonviolent despite beatings, kicks, and arrests.

On May 4th, less than a month after he had become a salt criminal, Gandhi was arrested in the night while sleeping in a tent a few miles from the scene of his crime. The prison authorities measured him and noted his height: five feet, five inches. To be sure they could identify him again for subsequent arrests, apparently, they recorded his birthmarks: a little scar on the right thigh, a small mole on the lower right eyelid, and a scar the size of a pea below the left elbow. Gandhi loved it in jail. "I have been quite happy and making up for arrears in sleep," he wrote Miss Slade. The prison goat was milked in his presence. (He drank no cow or buffalo milk but his wife Kasturbai had persuaded him, during a near-fatal illness, to take goat's milk. It helped, and he remained an addict for the rest of his life.)

Several days before his arrest, Gandhi had informed the Viceroy that, "God willing," he would, with some companions, raid the Dharsana Salt Works, 150 miles north of Bombay. God, it developed, was not willing. Mrs. Sarojini Naidu, the poet, substituted as leader of the raid. Twenty-five hundred volunteers participated. Before proceeding Mrs. Naidu warned them that they would be beaten "but," she said, "you must not resist; you must not even raise a hand or ward off a blow."

Webb Miller, the well-known correspondent of the United Press, who died in England during the second world war, was on the scene and described the event first in dispatches and then in his book, *I Found No Peace*. Manilal

Gandhi, second son of the Mahatma, advanced at the head of the marchers and approached the great salt pans which were surrounded by ditches and barbed wire and guarded by four hundred Surat policemen under the command of six British officers. "In complete silence," Miller writes, "the Gandhi men drew up and halted a hundred yards from the stockade. A picked column advanced from the crowd, waded the ditches, and approached the barbed-wire stockade." The officers ordered them to retreat but they continued to step forward. "Suddenly," the report reads, "at a word of command, scores of native policemen rushed upon the advancing marchers and rained blows on their heads with their steel-shod lathis [staves]. Not one of the marchers even raised an arm to fend off the blows. They went down like ten-pins. From where I stood I heard the sickening whack of the clubs on unprotected skulls. The waiting crowd of marchers groaned and sucked in their breath in sympathetic pain at every blow. Those struck down fell sprawling, unconscious or writhing with fractured skulls or broken shoulders. . . . The survivors, without breaking ranks, silently and doggedly marched on until struck down." When the first column was laid low, another advanced. "Although everyone knew," Webb Miller writes, "that within a few minutes he would be beaten down, perhaps killed, I could detect no sign of wavering or fear. They marched steadily, with heads up, without the encouragement of music or cheering or any possibility that they might escape injury or death. The police rushed out and methodically and mechanically beat down the second column. There was no fight, no struggle, the marchers simply walked forward until struck down." Another group of twenty-five advanced and sat down. "The police," Miller testifies, "commenced savagely kicking the seated men in the abdomen and testicles." Another column presented itself. Enraged, the police dragged them by their arms and feet and threw them into the ditches. "One was dragged to a ditch where I stood," Miller recorded; "the splash of his body doused me with muddy water. Another policeman dragged a Gandhi man to the ditch, threw him in, and belabored him over the head with his lathi. Hour after hour stretcher-bearers carried back a stream of inert, bleeding men."

A British officer took Mrs. Naidu's arm and said, "Sarojini Naidu, you are under arrest." She shook off his hand. "I will come," she said, "but don't touch me." Manilal Gandhi likewise submitted to arrest.

The raids and beatings continued for several days.

India was now free. Legally, technically, nothing had changed. India was still a British colony. But there was a difference and Rabindranath Tagore explained it. He told the *Manchester Guardian* of May 17, 1930, that "Europe has completely lost her former moral prestige in Asia. She is no longer regarded as the champion throughout the world of fair dealing and the exponent of high principle, but as the upholder of Western race supremacy and the exploiter of those outside her own borders. For Europe this is, in actual fact, a great moral defeat that has happened. Even though Asia is physically weak and unable to protect herself from aggression where her vital interests are menaced, nevertheless she can now afford to look down on Europe where before she looked up." Tagore attributed the achievement in India to Gandhi.

The Salt March and its aftermath did two things: it gave the Indians the conviction that they could lift the foreign yoke from their shoulders; it made the British aware that they were subjugating India. It was inevitable, after 1930, that India would some day refuse to be ruled, and, more important, that England would some day refuse to rule.

When the Indians allowed themselves to be beaten with batons and rifle butts and did not cringe they showed that England was powerless and India invincible. The rest was merely a matter of time.

## 17    The Half-Naked Fakír

Prime Minister Ramsay MacDonald was embarrassed to be the jailer of Gandhi. From all over the world and from his own country came a deluge of telegrams asking for the Mahatma's release. Mr. MacDonald and some of his Cabinet ministers could be faced with their public statements lauding Gandhi and favoring Indian home rule. Lord Irwin was more than embarrassed; civil disobedience had crippled his administration. Revenue dropped steeply. The police and military groaned under the superhuman assignment of maintaining law and order.

A Round Table Conference, attended by Indians who were the Viceroy's appointees, met in London late in November, 1930, and came to nothing; Congress, the only popular organization in India, was not represented. At its closing session on January 19, 1931, MacDonald expressed the hope that Congress would send delegates to the second Round Table Conference. But they were all in jail in India. Lord Irwin took the hint—or the command—and freed Gandhi, the Nehrus, father and son, and twenty other top Congressmen on January 25th, the eve of the Congress-proclaimed Independence Day. In appreciation of this conciliatory gesture, Gandhi wrote Irwin asking for an interview.

Irwin obliged. The first meeting took place on February 17th, at 2:30 P.M., and lasted three hours and forty minutes. "So the stage was set," writes Irwin's biographer, "for the most dramatic personal encounter between a Viceroy and an Indian leader in the whole seething history of the British raj."

It was more than dramatic. It was historic and decisive. Winston Churchill saw this better than anyone. He was revolted, he declared, by "the nauseating and humiliating spectacle of this one-time Inner Temple lawyer, now seditious fakir, striding half-naked up the steps of the Viceroy's palace, there to negotiate and parley on equal terms with the representative of the King-Emperor." (A fakir is an Indian mendicant monk.)

Churchill's anger and contempt, undisguised and ferocious, did not blur his vision. He grasped the basic fact which was not the state of the Mahatma's undress or his discarded profession but the equality he had acquired and was asserting in the parleys with Irwin. Gandhi had not come, like most of the Viceroy's visitors, to petition for favors. He came as the leader of a nation to negotiate "on equal terms" with the representative of another nation. The Salt March had demonstrated that England could not govern India against Gandhi. The British raj was at the mercy of the half-naked fakir, and Churchill felt nauseated. Churchill sensed that England was conceding India's independence in principle while temporarily withholding it in practice.

After many meetings and much wrangling, Irwin and Gandhi signed what Irwin's biographer called "The Delhi Pact" on March 5th. Two national statesmen had concluded a pact, a treaty, an agreed text. Civil disobedience would be canceled, prisoners released, and salt manufacture permitted on the sea-coast. Congress would attend the next Round Table Conference in London. Neither independence nor Dominion status was promised.

Within a few months, and certainly in the perspective of historic events, the terms of the Pact lost their significance. British spokesmen maintained that in the negotiations leading to it, Irwin had won the battle, and there is substance in the contention. Several Congressmen criticized the Mahatma for having failed to achieve a concrete fraction of independence. Another politician might have fought for more concessions. Gandhi was satisfied with the essence; he had established the foundation for a new relationship between India and Britain. Seventeen years later—a minute in the life of an ancient people—India would be independent. The Pact was a step, a means, not an end.

Emphasis on means gave Gandhi a broad perspective, patience, and equanimity. He could wait for dividends as long as the business operated on the right kind of principle.


## 18   In London in Minus Fours

Gandhi sailed from Bombay on the *S.S. Rajputana* at noon on August 29, 1931, accompanied by his youngest son, Devadas, his chief secretary, Mahadev Desai, who, he said, "out-Boswelled Boswell," Miss Slade, Pyarelal Nayyar, an aide, G. D. Birla, the textile millionaire, Pandit Malaviya, and Mrs. Naidu. Gandhi was proceeding as sole delegate of Congress to the second Round Table Conference in London. No other delegates were necessary since he spoke for the organization and for a considerable segment of vocal India.

In London from September 12th to December 5th, he stayed, most of the time, at Kingsley Hall, an East Settlement House, as guest of Muriel Lester, who had visited him in 1926. Mornings he took walks through the nearby slum areas and men and women on the way to work would smile at him and he engaged them in conversation and later came to their homes. Children called him "Uncle Gandhi" and sidled up to him and held his hand. One mischief-loving youngster called out, "Hey, Gandhi, where's your trousers?" The Mahatma had a good laugh.

He was wonderful newspaper copy, and journalists buzzed around him incessantly. One reporter questioned Gandhi about his dress. "You people," he replied, "wear plus-fours, mine are minus-fours." When he was invited to tea in Buckingham Palace with King George V and Queen Mary all England was agog over what he would wear. He wore the usual loincloth, sandals, a shawl, and his dangling dollar watch. Subsequently someone asked Gandhi whether he had had enough on. "The King," he replied, "had enough on for both of us."

He enjoyed himself everywhere. He had talks with Lord Irwin, wartime Prime Minister David Lloyd George, the Archbishop of Canterbury, Field Marshal Smuts, Bernard Shaw, and scores of others, and went down into the country near Reading to pay his respects to Colonel Maddock who had performed the appendectomy on him in Poona jail. Winston Churchill refused to see him.

He also addressed innumerable public meetings and spent two memorable week ends at Oxford. In these and in the private conversations he tried, above all else, to explain what he meant by the independence of India. He would cut India off "from the Empire entirely, from the British nation not at all, if I want India to gain and not to grieve. The Emperorship must go and I should love to be an equal partner with Britain sharing her joys and sorrows and an equal partner with the Dominions. But it must be a partnership on equal terms." He was describing precisely and with remarkable prevision the status free India assumed in the Commonwealth in 1948.

He went even further; he saw what many of his followers have not yet discerned. "Isolated independence is not the goal," he asserted. "It is voluntary interdependence." Liberated colonies so treasure their new-found independence they think it is a viable reality. But the law of nature, in love, friendship, work, progress, and security, is creative interdependence.

Everywhere he made friends by his charm, frankness, humanity, and accessibility. He even walked into the lion's den in Lancashire where his agitation for khadi and against foreign cloth had caused painful unemployment. At a meeting of the textile millworkers, one man said, "I am one of the unemployed, but if I was in India I would say the same thing that Mr. Gandhi is saying." A delightful photograph taken outside the Greenfield Mill at Darwen shows Gandhi wrapped in white homespun from neck to knee, for it was cold, and squeezed in among cheering, applauding women, one of whom, to his embarrassment, is holding his hand. He made friends even among those he hurt.

"I found that my work lies outside the Conference," he told a London audience. "This is the real Round Table Conference. . . . The seed which is being sown now may result in softening the British spirit and in preventing the brutalization of human beings."

Mahadev Desai's diaries show that the Mahatma often got to bed at 2 A.M., awoke at 3:45 A.M. for prayers, wrote letters and read papers, rested again from 5 to 6, and had no respite from then till the next morning at 1 or 2 A.M. Small wonder that he occasionally slept at sessions of the Conference. He did not give it his best.

The Round Table Conference was bound to fail. Lord Reading, a member of the British delegation, formulated the British purpose in one sentence: "I believe that the true policy between Britain and India is that we should in this country strive all we can to give effect to the views of India while preserving at the same time our own position, which we must not and cannot abandon." An irresistible force, India's yearning to be free, met an immovable object, Britain's wish to stay in India. That made agreement impossible.

The British government had assigned two Scotland Yard detectives to guard Gandhi in England. They were special policemen, giants in size, who usually protected royalty. They grew to like "the little man." Unlike most dignitaries, Gandhi did not keep them at arm's length or ignore them. He discussed public affairs with them and visited their homes. Before leaving England he requested that they be allowed to accompany him to Brindisi, Italy, whence he would sail for India. Their chief asked the reason why.

"Because they are part of my family," Gandhi replied.
From India he sent each a watch engraved "With love from M. K. Gandhi."

## 19 *Children of God*

"I have come back empty-handed," Gandhi told the mammoth crowd which received him at Bombay as he stepped down the gangplank on December 28th. But "judging by the warmth, cordiality, and affection displayed at the reception, one would think the Mahatma had returned with Swaraj in the hollow of his hand," Subhas Chandra Bose remarked caustically. He had returned with integrity unimpaired and good will abounding. "I am not conscious of a single experience throughout my three months in England and Europe," he reported, "that made me feel that after all East is East and West is West. On the contrary, I have been convinced more than ever that human nature is much the same, no matter under what clime it flourishes, and that if you approached people with trust and affection, you would have ten-fold trust and thousand-fold affection returned to you."

Exactly a week later he was in jail.

Lord Willingdon had replaced Irwin as Viceroy, and in October, 1931, a new government took office in England with Ramsay MacDonald as Prime Minister, to be sure, but Conservatives filling key posts. Sir Samuel Hoare was Secretary of State for India. Within several weeks, Emergency Powers Ordinances were proclaimed in Bengal, the United Provinces, and the Northwest Frontier Province, where Congress was charged with endeavoring to obstruct the British government by setting up a parallel government. "The question is," Sir Harry Haig, Home Member (Minister of Interior) of the Government of India declared, "whether the Congress is going to impose its will on the whole country."

Jawaharlal Nehru and many other leaders had already been imprisoned, and now Gandhi was lodged in Yeravda jail; he was soon joined by Vallabhbhai Patel, whom Gandhi had dubbed "Sardar" or noble man, and Mahadev Desai.

The Mahatma always obeyed the prison rules strictly as well as his own rule not to agitate from prison. Since he could not be a politician he concentrated on being the saint. Many the talks he had with Vallabhbhai and Mahadev on sacred subjects; sometimes other prisoners as well as British wardens and physicians participated.

After a while Gandhi began to write down his thoughts on God and the ideal conduct of man; these were later published as a little book called *Yeravda Mandir*. Mandir means temple. A jail where God is discussed and worshipped becomes a temple. "God is," Gandhi wrote.

The word *satya* means "truth," and it derives from *sat* which means "to be." *Sat* also denotes God. Therefore "Truth is God" and God is that which is. "He alone is," Gandhi noted, for "nothing else I see merely through the senses can or will persist."

Over the years Gandhi tried to prove the existence of God. "It is possible to reason out the existence of God to a limited extent," he ventured. "There is an orderliness in the Universe, there is an unalterable law governing everything and every being that exists or lives. It is not a blind law, for no blind law can govern the conduct of human beings. . . . That law then which governs all life is God. . . . I do dimly perceive that whilst everything around me is ever changing, ever dying, there is underlying all that change a living Power that is changeless, that holds all together, that creates, dissolves, and re-creates. That informing Power or spirit is God. . . . In the midst of death life persists, in the midst of untruth truth persists, in the midst of darkness light persists. Hence I gather that God is Life, Truth, and Love. He is Love. He is the supreme God."

But, suspecting the failure of this valiant rational effort, he conceded that "faith transcends reason. . . . If we could solve all the mysteries of the Universe, we would be co-equal with God. Every drop of ocean shares its glory but is not the ocean." By analogy, every human being partakes of the nature of God but is not God and cannot know what He is. "The safest course," the Mahatma advised, "is to believe in the moral government of the world and therefore in the supremacy of the moral law, the law of truth and love. . . ."

God preoccupied Gandhi but he never had a mystic experience, "never heard a voice, saw a vision, or had some recognized experience of God." Although non-Indian mystics, eager to pin their mysticism to a fixed point, occasionally attached themselves to Gandhi, he was not a mystic and disclaimed being one. "I have no special revelation of God's will," he insisted. He argued instead that "He reveals Himself daily to every human being, but we shut our ears to the 'still small voice.' . . . God never appears to you in person but in action."

Presently, in the prison silences of Yeravda Temple, the Mahatma heard that still small voice calling him to action. The result was the tensest fortnight in India's modern history. "To find a parallel for the anguish of September, 1932," Rajagopalachari wrote, "we have to go back to Athens twenty-three centuries ago when the friends of Socrates surrounded him in prison and importuned him to escape from death. . . . Socrates smiled at the suggestion . . . and preached the immortality of the soul."

Unafraid to die, certain that the soul never dies, the Mahatma undertook a fast unto death on an issue which to him was supremely religious. It concerned the Untouchables, the most miserable of the many miserable people in India.

An orthodox Hindu must not touch an untouchable or anything an untouchable touches. If by chance he does he purges himself by religiously prescribed ablutions. Even the shadow of an untouchable is regarded as unclean in some areas of India. Obviously, therefore, untouchables should not enter a Hindu temple. They inhabit the worst sections of the world's worst urban slums, and in villages they live on the lowest outskirts into which the filth and dirty waters drain, but it is the only water they can use, for the well is forbidden to them. It would be polluted.

The untouchables are outcastes in the Hindu sense in that they do not belong to the four Hindu castes, which are, from superior to inferior: the Brahmans or priests, the Kshatriyas or rulers and warriors, the Vaisyas or tradesmen and farmers, and the Sudras or laborers. Below these, but too low to stand even on the lowest rung of the Hindu social ladder, come the outcaste untouchables, Hindus outside the pale.

Centuries ago, castes and the thousands of subdivisions within each caste were professional, hereditary guilds. Thus Gandhi belonged to the Vaisya caste and to the Modh-Bania subcaste. Banias are traders, and the Gandhis, far back, were grocers. *Gandhi* means grocer. Tradition as well as the local authorities kept all adults within their own guilds so that higher castes could not lose caste by being flooded with members of lower castes, and low castes were not invaded by unemployed from above. This arrangement presumably gave each group the advantage of economic security, but it also subjected the individual to economic regimentation.

Though caste often performed this stabilizing economic function, its origin was political and its sanction religious. The Aryans, who came south from their Central Asian homelands thousands of years ago during the long, un-chronicled night before the dawn of history, gradually conquered India from the Indus River and the Himalaya Mountains down to the southern tip of the peninsula at Cape Comorin, and as they proceeded they tolerantly merged their own customs and ideas with the indigenous cultures—the product is the composite now known as Hinduism. Yet they made the native inhabitants their economic tools, retaining for themselves the profitable and glamorous tasks of governing and fighting. So great was the power of religion, however, that the Brahmans established themselves as the highest caste, higher than the rulers and warriors, and this chiefly because they were able to give the caste gradations a guarantee of stability by hallowing them with the mantle of religion. They clothed caste in a sacred formula of immutable fate: you are a Brahman or a Sudra or untouchable because of your conduct in a previous incarnation. Caste rank is thus preordained for this life and everyone must submit. But good conduct now can bring posthumous promotion or *vice versa*. A greedy Brahman might be reborn in the merchant class whereas a spiritual trader could return as a Brahman. A woman might become a man in the next incarnation, and *vice versa*. Some Hindus would like to feel that at rebirth they will still be members of the same family though their relationships might be altered; a husband and wife may be brother and sister, or sister and brother. Men with feminine propensities might turn to women, and the soul of a blood-thirsty Hindu could be reincarnated in an animal.

Some untouchables have tried, by accepting Christianity or Islam, to escape their dire, humiliating lot, but the fifty or sixty million of them bow to fate in the belief that they are doing penance for ancestral wickedness and in the hope of elevation in an incarnation yet to be. With only a few hundred exceptions, therefore, the untouchables of India continue segregated in their menial jobs of sweeping streets, scrubbing floors, cleaning lavatories, working leather, and doing other things which are under a caste-Hindu religious taboo. To this day, in the highly minute division of labor, a hospital nurse will not touch a bedpan or make a bed, and the orderly who makes the bed and brings the food tray would refuse the patient's request to pick up a piece of bandage from the floor, much less handle an object in the bathroom; those duties are the untouchable's. There is a social scale even within the untouchable community; in the home of a rich friend in Bombay, the untouchables who are his permanent servants will not clean lavatories lest it become known in their villages and degrade them. They go out into town to hire lower untouchables.

In contrast to the rigidity with which untouchables are held in their lowly place, the occupational barriers among caste Hindus began breaking down quickly in the nine-teenth century and in some areas earlier. Gandhi's grand-father and father, for instance, were not grocers, they were prime ministers. Today, a Brahman may be a taxi driver (yet if he is a farmer in certain districts he will not plow but pay a lower-caste Hindu to do it for him); a Vaisya may be a high government official or professor, and a Kshatriya or warrior may be employed as a bookkeeper.

But though the castes as professional groupings are dis-integrating under the impact of modern economic pressures, the social distinctions between them persist stubbornly. No matter how poor the Brahman or how plain his job, he will not permit his children to marry into a caste beneath them, nor will he welcome low-caste Hindus at his table.

In the early years of his Mahatmahood, Gandhi favored the caste system. "I consider the four divisions to be fun-damental, natural, and essential," he said in 1920, and on October 6, 1921, he wrote in *Young India,* "Prohibition against intermarriage and interdining is essential for the rapid evolution of the soul." This defense of an ignoble aspect of Hindu orthodoxy stands as a quotable charge against him, but he actually reversed himself in word and deed. "Restriction on intercaste dining and intercaste marriage," he declared on November 4, 1932, "is no part of the Hindu religion. Today, these two prohibitions are weakening Hindu society." In 1921 they were "essential," in 1932, debilitating. He was too observant, flexible, and honest to support the systematic discrimination which was fragmentizing and corrupting Hindu society.

An intimate experience probably helped to change his mind. In 1927, Gandhi's youngest son Devadas fell in love with Lakshmi, the daughter of C. Rajagopalachari and wished to marry her. But Rajagopalachari was a Brahman and Gandhi a Vaisya, and Gandhi objected to the intercaste marriage as well as to the love match. He was old-style enough to maintain, as innumerable educated Hindus still do, that matches made by parents are happier than those born of affection. But Devadas and the maid persisted, and finally the illustrious fathers agreed to sanction the union if the young folks still wanted one another after five years of separation. So they waited, painfully, until they were married with pomp in Poona on June 16, 1933, in the presence of both joyous fathers.

In subsequent years Gandhi refused to attend any but intercaste marriages. Indeed, having broken with Hindu orthodoxy, he travelled further and further away from it until he was able to say in the *Hindustan Standard* of January 4, 1946, "I therefore tell all boys and girls who want to marry that they cannot be married at Sevagram Ashram [to which Gandhi moved after he left Sabarmati] unless one of the parties is an untouchable." He had thus gone full circle from utter disapproval of intercaste marriages to approval of only intercaste marriages, and then to the climax of horror for orthodox Hindus: caste-outcaste marriages with his personal blessing. That he should nevertheless have had a growing following among Hindus is part of the miracle of Gandhi and a tribute to the tolerance of Hindus in the midst of their intolerance.

Greater wisdom showed Gandhi the evils of caste but his hostility to untouchability was emotional and appeared in childhood. "I used to laugh at my mother," he wrote in a letter to Charles Freer Andrews, "for making us bathe when we brothers touched any pariah." He played with an untouchable boy even after his beloved Putlibai forbade it. In South Africa some of his law clients and friends were untouchables, and he lodged one in his home. Returned to India, he attended a Bombay meeting in May, 1918, called to improve the condition of untouchables. On being introduced he asked, "Is there an untouchable here?" and when no hand was raised he refused to deliver his address. He had no sooner established himself at Sabarmati than he invited an untouchable father, mother, and their little daughter Lakshmi to dwell in it as members. The wealthy Bombay and Ahmedabad magnates thereupon withdrew their financial support of the ashram. Undeterred, Gandhi declared he would go live in a hut in the untouchable quarter. But one morning a man, later revealed as Ambalal Sarabhai, the biggest textile manufacturer in Ahmedabad, drove up in a car, put thirteen thousand rupees in bills in Gandhi's hand and departed. Still the women of the ashram refused to work in the kitchen with the untouchable woman. Hindus attach great importance to food, and her presence where it was prepared defiled everything the community ate. Even Kasturbai, accustomed as she was to her holy husband's idiosyncrasies, could not stomach this one. He appealed to her reason and generous nature, but the belief in untouchability resides in some remote nervous recess where, with racial intolerance, dogma, and color prejudice as its neighbors, it resists common sense and humaneness. He therefore told her that if this was a sin it was his for he was responsible and as a Hindu wife she must obey. These were terms she understood. The other ashram women followed her in acquiescing. But this did not end the troubles. One morning the Mahatma announced that he was adopting little Lakshmi as his daughter, and therefore as Kasturbai's daughter. The devout, semiliterate Kasturbai stood aghast and uncomprehending. In many ways, however, she had a more saintly, yogi character than her tempestuous spouse, and especially after he ceased being carnal, she accepted him as her teacher. Who was she to question the man of God? In her nerve tissue, nevertheless, the aversion to untouchables continued to twitch.

Over the years, many thousands of high-caste Hindus felt honored to come to the ashram to talk and eat with Gandhi. A few undoubtedly purged themselves on leaving, but most could not be such hypocrites. Untouchability lost some of its curse for them. The mass, however, could adore Gandhi and abhor untouchables.

Theoretically a barrier to contamination, untouchability contaminates those who practice it and the country that allows it. The degraders are dragged down morally, economically, and socially with those they degrade. The wholesale exodus of untouchables from Hinduism would forever blacken the conscience of Hindus without benefit to untouchables. Rather than acquiesce in such a defeat, which in any case was only the suggestion of a few of their leaders and enjoyed no prospect of wide acceptance, for the naïvely religious untouchables would be afraid to forfeit their chances of a better life in coming incarnations, Gandhi preferred "to sting the Hindu conscience into right religious action." That was the reason for his fast unto death.

In the great drama which impended, the protagonists were the Mahatma and Ambedkar. Dr. Bhimrao Ramji Ambedkar, the top untouchable leader, owned a powerful body and strong, stubborn, superior intellect. His grandfather and father had distinguished themselves by service in the British Army and through them he became known to the Gaekwar (Maharajah) of Baroda, who sent him on a scholarship to the Columbia University Law School in New York. His brilliant career as attorney lifted him into prominence and gave him acceptance as spokesman for the untouchables. As such he attended the Second Round Table Conference in London in September-December, 1931, and proposed a separate electorate for untouchables or, at least, the reservation of seats for untouchables inside the Hindu bloc in Indian legislatures. Gandhi opposed both as divisive, reactionary, and unfruitful.

Subsequently, however, the London authorities continued to labor on a constitution for India and before long it became known to Gandhi in Yeravda prison that the new statutes would provide not only for a separate Moslem electorate but for a separate electorate for the "Depressed Classes," as the British officially termed the untouchables. (Gandhi called them *Harijans,* which means Children of

God, and his new weekly was entitled *Harijan*.)

In 1909, the British had introduced separate electorates for Hindus and Moslems. In consequence, and as long as the British raj remained in India, a Moslem could vote only for a Moslem candidate, and a Hindu only for a Hindu. The mischief produced by this institution was incalculable because it made religious differences the deciding factor in every political contest. It was as though Catholics in England, the United States, and France could vote only for Catholic candidates to parliament and all other offices, and Protestants for only Protestant candidates, and Jews for only Jews. The central problem was to bridge the gulf between Hindus and Moslems and thereby make India a nation, but separate electorates, by closing the door to political intermingling, destroyed the bridge and widened the gulf.

Now in addition, England planned a separate electorate for the "Depressed Classes." Gandhi accordingly protested to Sir Samuel Hoare on March 11, 1932, and declared that if indeed the British created a separate untouchables electorate "I must fast unto death." This, he knew, would embarrass the authorities whose prisoner he was, "but for me the contemplated step is not a method, it is part of my being."

The minister replied to the prisoner saying no decision had yet been taken and before it was taken his views would be considered. No new development occurred until August 17, 1932, when Prime Minister Ramsay MacDonald pronounced in favor of separate electorates. The next day, Gandhi sent a letter to the Prime Minister which stated that "I have to resist your decision with my life." The fast, he wrote, would commence at noon, September 20th.

In a very long reply, dated 10 Downing Street, September 8, 1932, Mr. MacDonald expressed his "surprise and, let me add, my very sincere regret." Mr. Gandhi, the Prime Minister suggested, had misunderstood; they had considered his known devotion to untouchables. The new legislation, the Prime Minister explained, would enable the Depressed Classes to vote with the Hindu electorate on an equal footing. Is that not what the Mahatma desired? And in addition, during the next twenty years, they would, in a number of specified electoral districts, vote as untouchables and choose their own legislators. In other words, MacDonald emphasized, an untouchable will "have two votes." Surely their champion, Gandhi, would not object.

Gandhi's answer, sent to Downing Street from Yeravda Central Prison, argued that "the mere fact of the Depressed Classes having double votes does not protect them or Hindu society from being disrupted. . . . I should not be against even overrepresentation of the Depressed Classes. What I am against is their statutory separation, even in a limited form, from the Hindu fold so long as they choose to belong to it."

That ended the correspondence between prisoner and Prime Minister. Gandhi would fast. The division of India into two electorates was bad enough. He could not contemplate three Indias.

From all sides came letters, messages, and telegrams attempting to dissuade Gandhi. Many friends did not understand why he intended to die on this issue. Nehru, in jail, "felt annoyed with him," he writes in his autobiography, *Toward Freedom,* "for choosing a side issue for his final sacrifice. . . . I felt angry with him. . . ."

Gandhi was unmoved. He saw beyond legalisms and logic. True, MacDonald's project provided for a separate electorate and a joint Hindu-Harijan electorate. But the good psychological effect of the joint electorate would be erased by the separate one. Given a separate electorate, Harijan candidates and elected legislators would stress what divided them from caste Hindus. A political party machine would arise with a vested interest in perpetuating the rift between castes and outcastes; its political ammunition would be Hindu injustice, very ample ammunition indeed. Such a setup clashed with Gandhi's basic principles: harmony in diversity; love despite differences. Divisions invite collisions; separation breeds hate and violence in thought and action.

Gandhi was not fasting against Britain, he was fasting to remove the disabilities from Harijans so they would want to form a political unit with Hindus. His target was the Hindu community. MacDonald had affirmed that if the Hindus and Harijans agreed on a different and mutually satisfactory voting arrangement, Britain would accept it.

At 11:30 A.M., on September 20th, Gandhi took his last meal. It consisted of a glass of hot water with honey and lemon juice.

## 20  The Magician

On the day he commenced his fast, Gandhi awoke at 2:30 A.M. and wrote a letter to Rabindranath Tagore. "This is early morning 3 o'clock Tuesday," he began. "I enter the fiery gates at noon. If you can bless the effort, I want it." He also invited Tagore's criticism "if your heart condemns my action. I am not too proud to make an open confession of my blunder, whatever the cost of the confession, if I find myself in error." But if he approved, Gandhi craved his blessing. "It will sustain me," the Mahatma said humbly.

Others might not understand, but Tagore knew India; Gandhi respected his views and would listen to them. Just as Gandhi was about to seal the letter, a telegram arrived from Tagore. "It is worth sacrificing precious life," it read, "for the sake of India's unity and her social integrity. . . . I fervently hope we will not callously allow such national tragedy to reach its extreme length."

Gandhi now added a P.S. thanking him for "your loving and magnificent wire. It will sustain me in the midst of the storm I am about to enter."

That evening Tagore addressed his school at Shantiniketan: "A shadow is darkening today over India like a shadow cast by an eclipsed sun. . . . Mahatmaji, who through his life of dedication has made India his own in truth, has commenced his vow of supreme self-sacrifice." He explained the fast: "Each country has its own geography where the spirit dwells and where physical force can never conquer even an inch of ground. Those rulers who come from the outside must remain outside the gates." England did not rule the soul of India. "But the Great Soul . . . continues his dominion even when he is physically no longer present. . . . The penance which Mahatmaji has taken upon himself is not a ritual but a message to all India and to the world. . . . No civilized society can thrive upon victims whose humanity has been permanently mutilated . . . we insult our own humanity by insulting man where he is helpless. . . . Against that deep-seated moral weakness in our society Mahatmaji has pronounced his ultimatum." It was not a side show. Gandhi was fasting to save the soul of India.

Immediately, Hindu leaders gathered in Bombay to confer with Harijan leaders, notably Ambedkar. Agelong Hindu cruelty to his unhappy brethren filled Ambedkar with anger and spite. If anybody in India could have contemplated Gandhi's death with equanimity, he was the man. He called the fast "a political stunt." At the conference, he faced the greatest Hindu minds, and he must have derived sweet pleasure watching them court him to save the life of their beloved Mahatma.

The object of the Hindu conferees was a joint electorate which would nevertheless satisfy Ambedkar's wish for unfettered Harijan representatives in the legislature. He contended that if Harijans were jointly elected by Harijan and Hindu voters—as Gandhi insisted—the Harijans would become Hindu stooges and hesitate to air their grievances lest the Hindus defeat them in the next election.

To meet Ambedkar's legitimate apprehension, Sir Tej Bahadur Sapru, the eminent jurist, proposed something new in India: primaries. The Harijan candidates for some seats in the legislature would be selected in private consultation between Hindus and untouchables. But the remainder of the candidates for the seats reserved to Harijans —Gandhi had accepted reserved Harijan seats the day before the fast—would not be on the slate; they would be nominated in primaries in which only Harijans voted. For each seat there would be a panel of three Harijans, and in the final election Hindus would vote for one of them. That would enable the Harijans to nominate their bravest, most outspoken champions, and the Hindus could never defeat them.

Ambedkar examined the scheme slowly, minutely. He left the conference for hours to study it with untouchable colleagues. Then he came back and tentatively accepted.

Now the problem was Gandhi. Sapru, Jayakar, Rajagopalachari, Devadas Gandhi, Rajendra Prasad, and Birla took the midnight train from Bombay to Poona and appeared before Gandhi at 7 A.M. on the second morning of the fast. Gandhi was already weak. He listened to the plan, asked questions, but remained noncommittal though receptive. He wanted to see it in writing, and he wished to talk with Ambedkar and Mr. M. C. Rajah, a pro-Gandhian Harijan in the legislature.

The next morning, Gandhi criticized the Sapru proposal. Why make a distinction between two sets of Harijan candidates? Why not have all candidates nominated in the all-Harijan primaries? Why should any Harijans be under a political debt to Hindus?

Ambedkar arrived in Gandhi's prison in the afternoon. He did most of the talking. He declared himself ready to help save the Mahatma's life but "I want my compensation," he said.

Gandhi had commenced to sink. The fast was affecting him badly. In previous fasts, he had taken water on the hour. Now he drank it irregularly. In previous fasts, massage moderated his aches. This time he refused massage. He was very agitated. Sharp pains racked his wasting body. He had to be moved to the bathroom on a stretcher. The least movement and sometimes speaking gave him nausea.

When Ambedkar said, "I want my compensation," Gandhi propped himself up painfully on an elbow and spoke for several minutes. He mentioned his devotion to untouchables. He discussed the Sapru plan point by point, and stated his objection: why not have all Harijan candidates nominated by Harijans only? Then he subsided, exhausted, on his pillow.

Ambedkar was delighted. He had expected to be put under pressure, in the presence of the dying Mahatma, to recede from his position. Instead, Gandhi was offering him more than he had tentatively accepted. Ambedkar accordingly welcomed Gandhi's improvements on the Sapru text.

Later that day, Mrs. Gandhi was transferred from Sabarmati Prison to Yeravda Prison. As she walked slowly toward her husband, she shook her head reprovingly from side to side and said, "Again the same story, eh?" He smiled. Her company cheered him. He permitted her to massage him and then accepted professional massage more for her sake than because he wanted it.

Friday, September 23rd, Dr. Gilder, the heart specialist, arrived from Bombay and together with prison physicians diagnosed the prisoner's condition as dangerous. Blood pressure was alarmingly high. (Gandhi's blood pressure always rose when big decisions were pending.) Death might come at any moment.

All day Ambedkar bargained with the Hindu negotiators. He presented new demands embodying his "compensation."

1. Prime Minister MacDonald's award had given the untouchables a total of 71 seats in the provincial legislatures. Ambedkar asked for 197.

2. Sapru had suggested a panel of three Harijan candidates for every seat. Gandhi suggested five; Ambedkar two. The fewer the nominees in the primaries the more easily Ambedkar could control them.

3. Finally, there was the question of a referendum in which Harijan voters would decide when the reserved seats for Harijans would be abolished and all distinction between Harijans and Hindus erased. Gandhi wanted it in five years, Ambedkar in fifteen.

Late Friday, Ambedkar visited Gandhi again. It was a hot sultry day. Gandhi lay on a white cot in the prison yard under a spreading mango tree. Not a leaf stirred. Gandhi's blood pressure had risen still higher. He could not speak above a whisper. Ambedkar bargained hard. No decision was reached.

Saturday, the fifth day of the fast, might, the doctors agreed, be the last day of his life. All morning, Ambedkar wrangled with the Hindus and at noon he appeared at the Mahatma's side. He reported that a compromise had been reached between the 71 seats offered by MacDonald and the 197 demanded by him. The figure would be 147. Gandhi approved. They had also compromised on the size of the panel.

One disagreement remained—on how long the political distinction between Hindus and Harijans in elections would continue. Ambedkar had come down to ten years. Gandhi would not budge from five.

The conferees met again and found Ambedkar adamant. Now Rajagopalachari did something which probably saved Gandhi's life. Without consulting Gandhi, he and Ambedkar agreed that the time of the abolition of the electoral difference between Hindus and Harijans would be determined in further discussion. This might make a referendum unnecessary.

Rajagopalachari rushed to the jail and explained the new arrangement to Gandhi.

"Will you repeat it?" said Gandhi. He was faint.

Rajagopalachari repeated it.

"Excellent," he whispered.

That Saturday, the Yeravda Pact, as Indian history knows it, was drafted and signed by the chief Hindu and Harijan negotiators.

The pact, however, was no pact and Gandhi refused to abandon his fast until the British government officially accepted it in place of the original MacDonald scheme. The text was wired to London. But it was Sunday, and most of the members of the government had left town. MacDonald was attending the funeral of an aunt in Sussex.

On hearing of the agreement in Poona, MacDonald returned hastily to 10 Downing Street. With Sir Samuel Hoare and Lord Lothian he studied the text till midnight.

Meanwhile, Gandhi's life was ebbing away. He told Kasturbai how to distribute his few personal belongings that lay around the cot. Tagore arrived from Calcutta and sang some songs which soothed the dying prisoner.

Monday morning, the British government announced in London and New Delhi that it had accepted the Yeravda Pact. At 5:15 P.M. Gandhi broke his fast by drinking a glass of orange juice which Kasturbai handed him.

In the six days of the "Epic Fast," as it came to be called, the important events did not take place in the prison yard, or in the room where Ambedkar made the Hindus pay, or in London. They happened throughout India. Nehru, who at first felt angry with Gandhi for fasting on the untouchable issue, soon saw the light. "Then," his autobiography records, "came the news of the tremendous upheaval all over the country. . . . What a magician, I thought, was this little man sitting in Yeravda Prison, and how well he knew how to pull the strings that pulled the people's hearts."

A Hindu change of heart was Gandhi's purpose in fasting. "No patched-up agreement between caste Hindus and rival Depressed Class leaders will answer the purpose," he stated five days before the fast commenced. "The agreement to be valid has to be real. If the Hindu mass mind is not yet ready to banish untouchability root and branch it must sacrifice me without the slightest hesitation." So as he lay waning he looked beyond the negotiations to the living reality of Hindu relations with untouchables.

The news of the fast permeated India. Those who read told those who could not read, "The Mahatma is fasting."

"Why is Mahatmaji fasting?"

"Because we Hindus close our temples to untouchables and treat them badly."

The cities buzzed with excitement. Peasants marketing in the cities carried the reports to the villages. India's ear was cocked for more news. "Mahatmaji is sinking." "Mahatmaji is dying." "We must hurry." It was evil to prolong Gandhi's agony. He was a slice of God, God's messenger on earth. The mass relationship to him was a highly emotional one, transcending logic. At the very beginning of fast week, the famous Kalighat Temple of Calcutta and the Ram Mandir of Benares, citadels of Hindu orthodoxy, were thrown open to untouchables for the first time in the thousands of years of Hindu history. In Bombay, a women's organization organized a poll in front of seven big Hindu temples with ballot boxes watched by volunteers. Worshippers cast 24,797 votes for the admission of Harijans, 445 against. Immediately, temples in which no Harijan foot had ever trod were opened to all. In Allahabad, twelve temples theretofore inaccessible to untouchables opened their doors to them on the first day of Gandhi's fast. In the native states of Baroda, Kashmir, Bhor, and Kolhapur, temple discrimination was stopped. The newspapers printed the names of hundreds of other temples that did likewise.

In Delhi, Caste Hindus and Harijans demonstratively fraternized in the streets. At the strictly Hindu Benares University, Principal Dhruva, with numerous Brahmans, dined publicly with numerous street cleaners, cobblers, and scavengers. Hindu pupils shared benches formerly reserved for untouchables. Roads and streets were opened to Harijans. Many villages and small towns allowed untouchables to use the common water wells.

Mrs. Swarup Rani Nehru, Jawaharlal's very orthodox mother, let it be known that she had accepted food from the hand of an untouchable. Thousands of prominent Hindu women followed her example. In villages and towns throughout India thousands of organizations adopted resolutions promising to stop and combat anti-Harijan discrimination. Telegraphed copies of these resolutions began to form a man-high heap in Gandhi's prison yard. A mother hovering over the crib of a tender child in a high-temperature crisis could be no more anxious than the India that watched the white cot of the sinking Mahatma. No mystic himself, he affected others mystically. Reason withdrew; passionately, frantically—because the end might have come at any moment—Hindus were reacting with one throbbing wish: he must not die.

During the six-day fast, weddings were postponed, and most Hindus refrained from going to cinemas, theaters, and restaurants. A spirit of reform, penance, and self-purification swept the land. The magician was also a musician with an artist's genius to play on the heartstrings of the inner man.

"No one shall be regarded as an untouchable by reason of his birth," the Yeravda Pact said. Devout Hindus, with large religious followings, signed that statement. It marked a religious reformation, a psychological revolution, a purge of Hinduism's millennial sickness. It was food for India's moral health. No cold political agreement between Gandhi and Ambedkar, without a fast, would have achieved such a result.

The "Epic Fast" improved Harijan conditions permanently and snapped a chain that stretched back into antiquity and had enslaved tens of millions. Links of the chain remain. *Harijan* magazine of June 14, 1952, reported: "In Parli, near Natham, a Harijan youth who refused to take tea in a coconut shell and insisted on being served in a glass tumbler was kicked and shoed on the head by a caste-Hindu who was subsequently convicted and fined. . . . In Kottagudi, a village barber who refused a haircut to a Harijan boy was charged by the Police and convicted by the Sub-Magistrate. But later, the Harijans were summoned by the caste-Hindus . . . and warned against using the service of this barber on pain of a collective fine being imposed on them. . . . In Kidaripatti, the Harijans are not allowed to take the corpses of their dead through the public footpath, or to ride through the village streets on bicycles. . . . At Kelavaloo, the Harijans take water from a dirty pond in which men bathe and the cattle are washed."

Such cases are legion. Visceral prejudices do not die in a day or a decade. But the fast transformed antiuntouchable discrimination from a religious duty into a moral sin and wrote into life a bill of Harijan rights.

Gandhi was pleased. Five days after the end of the fast he was spinning and writing for many hours and his weight had gone up to 99 and three fourths pounds. "The fast," he said in a letter to Miss Slade, "was really nothing compared with the miseries that the outcastes have undergone for ages. And so I continue to hum 'God is great and merciful.'"

He remained in prison.

## 21  Personal

On May 8, 1933, Gandhi, still in prison, undertook a three weeks' fast because an attractive young American woman had caused some backsliding in the ashram. The government released him on the first day; remembering the Harijan "Epic Fast," it wanted no dead Mahatma on its hands. But he stood the fast very easily; spirit and mind were relaxed.

He now gave Sabarmati Ashram to a group of untouchables and established headquarters at Wardha, a small town near the geographic center of India. Later he settled in Sevagram village, a few miles from Wardha. In November, 1933, he left on a ten-month tour for Harijan welfare and visited every province of India without once returning home. From 1934 to 1939, he devoted himself to the promotion of spinning, basic education, the spread of Hindi and Hindustani as the national language, right diet, nature cure, as well as the relief of outcastes and the affairs of Congress. The chief organizer of the Congress party was Sardar Vallabhbhai Patel, a lawyer with a steel-trap mind and marvelous memory for names who could be friendly and firm and was at home in the maze of interlocking, feuding provincial, business, class, caste, religious, and political interests over and around which the Congress formed a kind of big flapping tent. The chief Congress propagandist was Jawaharlal Nehru, handsome, sensitive, morbid, who called himself a socialist and attracted the youth and intellectuals by his eloquence and demeanor. Gandhi gave the party some attention but social uplift absorbed more of him. In his magazine, he published formulas for animal manures and prescriptions for the cure of snake bites and malaria. Or he expatiated on the nutritional value of the lowly peanut. Peanuts were politics as political as parties, elections, and conferences. Nothing Indian was alien to him. He was India and India claimed him as her own. All questions and problems were brought to him and his opinions often had the authority of laws and of high court verdicts. He lived without a wall, accessible to everybody; he ate, slept, walked, talked, worked, read, and spun in public, and all his acts and thoughts were public property. If he allowed a sick, suffering calf to be put to painless death with a doctor's injection the protest mail was heavy and ferocious. He insisted he had done right. Another controversy, which even went to the length of threats of physical assault, raged around Gandhi's comment on being told that a textile manufacturer had rounded up sixty stray dogs on his industrial premises and killed them. "What else could be done?" Gandhi had remarked. This was offensive to Hinduism, his critics yelled. He filled whole issues of his magazine with their screeching letters. They charged, among other things, that he had succumbed to Western inhumanity. His reply stung. "The ideal of humanity in the West," he began softly, "is perhaps lower, but their practice of it is very much more thorough than ours. We rest content with a lofty ideal and are slow or lazy in its practice."

The problem of child widows also concerned him. Parents would marry their baby daughters to baby sons of other families, or even to old men, and if the husband died in infancy or of senility, the widow, who might be age three or six, could not, under Hindu law, remarry. "The existence of girl widows," Gandhi wrote, "is a blot upon Hinduism. . . . I consider the remarriage of virgin widows not only desirable but the bounden duty of all parents who happen to have such widowed daughters." To bigoted Hindus who contended that this would constitute a religiously-proscribed second marriage, Gandhi retorted, "They were never married at all." His objection to girl widows was that they were "strangers to love," and every human being must have love.

But physical love should be restrained; frequent sexual intercourse, he believed, has a debilitating effect on Indians. When Margaret Sanger visited him in December, 1935, to enlist his decisive aid for birth control in India, she received no encouragement. "Even assuming," he said on one occasion, "that birth control by artificial aids is justifiable under certain conditions"—a valuable admission—"it seems utterly impracticable of application among the millions" to whom a penny is a day's income. He did see the need of limiting India's population. "If I could find a way of stopping procreation in a civil and voluntary manner whilst India remains in her present miserable state I would do so today," he wrote Charles F. Andrews. The manner he favored was mental discipline: "Self-control is the surest and only method of regulating the birth rate." His one realistic contribution to the problem of checking population increases was late marriage, no earlier than twenty-one for women and the mid-twenties for men. He tried to keep his sons from marrying early. But an increase of five million mouths per year in the 1940's and 1950's, surely excessive in Indian conditions since it canceled out even the considerable economic progress of the postindependence period and thus conduced to frustration, could not be eliminated by raising the minimum age of marriage a few years.

In denying that "sexual indulgence for its own sake"—and not for procreation—"is a human necessity," Gandhi forgot his own youth and young manhood. Even later, though he remained chaste from thirty-seven till assassination, sex did not die. "My darkest hour," the ripe Mahatma of sixty-seven revealed in *Harijan* of December 26, 1936, "was when I was in Bombay a few months ago. It was an hour of temptation. Whilst I was asleep I suddenly felt as though I wanted to see a woman. Well a man who has tried to rise superior to the instinct for nearly forty years was bound to be intensely pained when he had this frightful experience. I ultimately conquered the feeling, but I was face to face with the blackest moment of my life and if I had succumbed to it, it would have meant my absolute undoing." Most persons are incapable of such self-revelation and would think it unnecessary, but he wanted the world to know the truth about him—his autobiography is entitled *Experiments in Truth*—and the truth was the whole truth which, he hoped, would be a lesson to others. "As I have all along contended that what is possible for one is possible for all," he said, "my experiments have not been conducted in the closet, but in the open."

The Mahatma's preoccupation with all kinds of intimate personal and social questions brought to his ever-open ashram door all manner of freaks, quacks, cranks, and crusaders longing for approval of their cracked or serious schemes. He also received visits from friends, acquaintances, political associates, and strangers who asked his consent to marry or separate, for he was adopted father, "Bapu," to a host of Indians. Why they should have thought he knew what was best for them and why they accepted advice that often had painful results is a puzzle in adulation. He himself had been a far from perfect husband and father. A foreigner once asked him, and only a foreigner would have asked, "How is your family?"

"All of India is my family," Gandhi replied. It made him rather impersonal toward his wife and children. A tension had marked his early relations with Kasturbai, but with age it gradually waned and they became a model couple, she the acme of service, he the paragon of consideration. She never behaved like Mrs. Gandhi, never accepted any privileges, never shirked the hardest work, and never seemed to notice the small group of adoring young and middle-aged female disciples who interposed themselves between her and her illustrious husband. During the week I spent with Gandhi in 1942, I never heard her say a single word to him nor did he speak to her. At meals and prayers she sat slightly behind his left shoulder fanning him solicitously and always looking at him. He rarely glanced at her, yet he wanted her nearest to him, and there appeared to be perfect understanding between them. It was obvious that though she was the shadow of the Mahatma she was also herself, and a very remarkable self, strong-willed, detached, observant. Her sunken face, straight thin mouth, and square jaw spelled suffering and dedication as well as determination. She never surrendered to him, and he seemed to enjoy it. "Ba," he once stated referring to Kasturbai as "Mother," "takes tea in spite of the fact that she lives with me." She likewise defied him and drank coffee. "I would even lovingly prepare it for her," he added. He grew to love her.

But he never quite learned to be a father to his sons. Expecting them to be junior saints, he denied them a formal education on the ground that character was more precious than learning and public service than a profession. They resented it. His oldest son Harilal became a dissolute, profligate drunkard, drifted away from his own wife and children, and, no doubt to pain the Mahatma, underwent conversion to Islam under the name of Abdulla. Manilal, Gandhi's second born, accepted undue paternal punishment and discipline in the self-abnegating spirit of his ascetic father and, unlike the rebel Harilal, sought to come close to his father's ideal by walking in his footsteps as a leader of the popular resistance to Prime Minister Malan's modern persecution of colored peoples in South Africa. Ramdas lived quietly in a small provincial Indian town managing a branch firm's business. Alone Devadas, the youngest son, stayed near the father, serving as secretary when invited but sometimes observing that the Mahatma was more affectionate as a grandfather. Perhaps the explanation is that Gandhi had an impersonal concept of immortality. "But may not an artist or a poet or a great genius leave a legacy of his genius to posterity through his children?" somebody asked.

"Certainly not," the Mahatma replied. "He will have more disciples than he can ever have children." He loved many children and believed in their goodness; "evil comes in only when they become older." I saw him make funny eyes at children in the ashram and pinch them tenderly. "She is my relaxation," he said about one infant he fondled in my presence. There is a delightful photograph of Gandhi rubbing noses with a babe in arms and another of him striding rapidly after a grandchild, the son of Ramdas, as they hold on to the opposite ends of a stick.

Neither young nor old stood in awe of Gandhi, and personal relations with him inside and outside the ashram were simple, direct, and friendly. He answered every letter in his voluminous correspondence, and never formally. Whenever people came with their private troubles he patiently soothed and smoothed. During the fateful negotiations with the British government in 1946, when colleagues and cabinet ministers were competing for his time, I saw him pace up and down his porch for a quarter of an hour talking

to a crippled young woman and then for an equal period
with a young man, and when I inquired I was told by an
aide that they were an untouchable couple whose relationship had spoiled and Gandhi was trying to patch it. He
gave and received endless love. There was in him something feminine. He often compared himself to a mother and
spoke of having been "widowed." "I hope you have not
missed the woman in me," he once wrote Mrs. Naidu. He
was fastidiously clean, studiously economical, and very
kind. The capacity for suffering and identification, his spinning and nonviolence probably contained elements of the
feminine. He liked to tend the sick and nurse the weak but
spurned such care himself. He looked very male and had
a man's steel strength of body and will, yet he was also
sweetly gentle and softly tender; firm yet caressing, adamant yet yielding, brave yet meek. He had the might of a
dictator but the mind of a democrat and therefore preferred
to conquer with affection rather than power. What he won
with iron he wrapped in down. Intuition was the ally of
his intellect, indeed sometimes guided or superseded it.
This combination of masculine and feminine qualities
seamlessly, harmoniously welded together made Gandhi
intricate and attractive, and supplies an important clue to
his personal life and public work.

## 22 Jesus Christ and Mahatma Gandhi

Among those who came to sit at Gandhi's feet were Christian missionaries. He loved Jesus, and Hindu bigots even
accused him of being a secret Christian. He considered
this "both a libel and a compliment—a libel because there
are men who believe me to be capable of being secretly
anything . . . a compliment in that it is a reluctant ac-

knowledgment of my capacity for appreciating the beauties of Christianity."

Always tolerant and fair-minded, Gandhi doubted that only the sacred Hindu Vedas were the revealed word of God. "Why not the Bible and the *Koran?*" he asked. He recoiled from rivalry between religions. In 1942, when I was his house guest, I noticed the one decoration on the mud walls of his little hut: a black-and-white print of Jesus Christ under which was written, "He Is Our Peace." I asked him about it. "You are not a Christian," I said.

"I am a Christian and a Hindu and a Moslem and a Jew," Gandhi replied. That made him a better Christian than most Christians.

Gandhi presented a perplexing problem to Christian divines in India: He, a Hindu, was the world's most Christlike person. "And so," commented Dr. E. Stanley Jones, a prominent American missionary who spent many years in India and many hours in communion with Gandhi, "one of the most Christlike men in history was not called a Christian at all."

"God," Dr. Stanley Jones declared, "uses many instruments, and He may have used Mahatma Gandhi to Christianize unchristian Christianity." Gandhi's message to Christians everywhere is that twentieth-century man can be a Christian. Mr. S. K. George, a Syrian Christian of India and lecturer at Bishop's College, Calcutta, wrote a book entitled, *Gandhi's Challenge to Christianity* and dedicated it "To Mahatma Gandhi Who Made Jesus and His Message Real to Me." The Reverend K. Matthew Simon, of the Syrian Christian Church of Malabar, India, said of Gandhi, "It was his life that proved to me more than anything else that Christianity is a practicable religion even in the twentieth century."

During many years of tender friendship, Charles Freer Andrews, the British missionary, and Gandhi grew so close that the Mahatma said of him, "He is more than a blood brother to me." Gandhi called him "Charlie," and he addressed Gandhi as "Mohan." "I do not think I can claim a deeper attachment to anyone than to Mr. Andrews," Gandhi wrote. The Hindu saint found no better soul kin than Andrews, the Christian; the Christian missionary found no better Christian than Gandhi, the Hindu.

In South Africa, for a moment, Gandhi thought of becoming a Christian. But there were questions that found no satisfactory answers. Why, he asked the Christians who were trying to convert him, did God have only one son? If He had one, why not another? In Hinduism, there have been a number of human incarnations of the Almighty. Why can I go to Heaven and attain salvation only as a Christian, Gandhi wondered. Was Heaven reserved for Christians? Was God a Christian? "I do believe," he said years later in India, "that in the other world there are neither Hindus, nor Christians, nor Moslems."

At Sabarmati and Sevagram too, missionaries sitting on the floor of his hut attempted to convert him to Christianity. He, speaking softly, attempted to do the same for them. (But why enroll a saint in a church?)

In these seminars, Gandhi occasionally chided the missionaries for making Christians of hungry Indians whom they fed and of sick Indians whom they healed. "Make us better Hindus," he pleaded. Gandhi could have converted many Christians to Hinduism. At a hint from him, Miss Slade and others would have become Hindus. He just told them to be good Christians.

In the end Gandhi embraced Christ but rejected Christianity. He formulated his attitude most clearly at the Y.M.C.A. in Colombo, Ceylon, in 1927. "If then I had to face only the Sermon on the Mount and my own interpretation of it," he declared, "I should not hesitate to say, 'Oh, yes, I am a Christian.' . . . But negatively I can tell you that much of what passes as Christianity is a negation of the Sermon on the Mount." He added a barb: "And please mark my words," Gandhi continued. "I am not speaking at the present moment of the Christian conduct. I am speaking of the Christian belief, of Christianity as it is understood in the West."

He threw a little more light on this view when I stayed with him in 1946. "Paul," he said, "was not a Jew, he was a Greek, he had an oratorical mind, a dialectical mind, and he distorted Jesus. Jesus possessed a great force, the love force, but Christianity became disfigured when it went to the West. It became the religion of kings." This thrust reflected his deepening disappointment with Western civilization. Observing the world's descent into war during the

1930's, Gandhi grew increasingly critical of the West and increasingly pacifist. He was never a complete pacifist, never a Tolstoyan absolutist in the sense of a person who would not countenance war under any circumstances. But to those who wondered why he supported the First World War yet refused to support the more justifiable Second World War against German Nazism, Italian fascism, and Japanese militarism, he might have replied that he was different and the world was different. He had more faith in nonviolence and less faith in the West. He saw fascism, Stalinism, war, crime, and corruption as related demonstrations of the triumph of Western violence over Christian morals, and he felt, therefore, that violence could not cure the evils that violence had produced. As a politician whose country faced invasion, Gandhi might not have permitted himself the luxury of such long-range perspectives (which is probably why he promised to remain "outside the official world" even in independent India) but as a superpolitician with spiritual eyes he saw that mankind would destroy itself if it did not take the long, therapeutic view. On the threshold of war there is always cogent justification for entering it. It is when the seeds of strife are being sown by greed and blown about by hate and stupidity that the Gandhian strategy can be applied.

Gandhi's nonviolence was first of all a creed of personal ethics which included truth, love, service, scrupulous methods and means, nonhurting by deed or word, tender tolerance of differences, and desirelessness or, at least, moderation in the pursuit of material things.

Gandhian nonviolence, secondly, is a technique for the prevention of conflict between races, communities, and countries. "Turn the searchlight inward," he repeatedly urged; perhaps the fault is partly yours. Adjudicate, negotiate, arbitrate, he begged, otherwise one interreligious brawl or one race riot will immediately create fuel for another, and one war will generate the venoms, fears and military designs which make a second and third more likely. Violence is self-perpetuating.

These are simple truths. Gandhi knew that. I suggested to him in 1946 that he ought to preach peace to the West. "Why does the West need me to tell them that two times two are four?" he wondered. Apparently the Western brain has grasped this arithmetic but the Western conscience and heart cannot draw the practical conclusions from it. Hence Gandhi's criticism of the Christian world. But neither was he blind to the faults of India. "I have unfinished work here," he stated in discussing a visit to the West.

"We have too many men of science, too few men of God. We have grasped the mystery of the atom and rejected the Sermon on the Mount." This was not Gandhi speaking, but General Omar N. Bradley, chairman of the Joint Chiefs of Staff of the United States armed forces, in a speech in Boston on November 10, 1948. "Ours," Bradley continued, "is a world of nuclear giants and ethical infants. We know more about war than we know about peace, more about killing than we know about living."

Gandhi knew nothing about killing, but had found the secret of happy, useful living. He was a nuclear infant and an ethical giant. He rejected the atom because he had accepted Christ's Sermon on the Mount. He was a Christian and a Hindu and a Moslem and a Jew. Who else is? Perhaps that it why it was a Hindu who became "the spokesman for the conscience of mankind." Since he always listened to the commands of his own conscience he could speak for, and to, the conscience of others.

## 23 Winston Churchill Versus Mohandas Gandhi

The day the Second World War started, Great Britain took India into the conflict by proclamation without consultation. India protested loudly against this additional humiliating proof of her impotence. But the very next day Gandhi boarded a train to Simla, the summer capital, and wept in an interview with Lord Linlithgow, the British Viceroy. "As I was picturing before him the House of Parliament and the Westminster Abbey and their possible destruction," Gandhi reported, "I broke down. I have become disconsolate. In the secret of my heart I am in perpetual quarrel with God that He should allow such things to go on."

Hitlerism, he said, "means naked ruthless forces reduced to an exact science and worked with scientific precision," and "I have come to the conclusion that Herr Hitler is responsible for the war." "My sympathy for England and France," he explained, "is not the result of momentary emotion. . . ." When France surrendered to the Nazis and England's life hung by the Royal Air Force, Gandhi soberly predicted that "Britain will die hard and heroically even if she has to. We may hear of reverses, but we shall not hear of demoralization." His respect for the virtues of the British people remained high throughout the war. "I do not want England to be defeated or humiliated," he declared in a speech to the All-India Congress Committee on September 15, 1940. "I have therefore nothing but good wishes for your country and Great Britain," Gandhi wrote in a letter to President Roosevelt, dated July 1, 1942, which he gave me for delivery.

By 1942, the Japanese had swept swiftly through Southeast Asia to the borders of India and threatened to invade. Gandhi stood firm against them. "If the Japanese come, how are we to resist them nonviolently?" he was asked.

"Neither food nor shelter is to be given," Gandhi replied in the June 14, 1942, *Harijan,* "nor any dealings to be established with them. They should be made to feel that they are not wanted. . . . The people . . . must evacuate the infested place in order to deny compulsory service to the enemy." Earlier, when Mr. Takoaka, a member of the Japanese Parliament, asked him for a message for the Japanese party which operated under the slogan of "Asia for the Asiatics," Gandhi refused, saying, "I do not subscribe to the doctrine of Asia for the Asiatics if it is meant as an anti-European combination."

For the duration, Gandhi remained anti-Japanese, anti-Nazi, anti-Mussolini, and pro-British, pro-French, pro-American. Affected by Nehru's wartime devotion to Generalissimo and Madame Chiang Kai-shek and the Soviet Union, Gandhi also made statements in support of China and Russia. "It is not because I love the British nation and hate the Germans," he asserted. "I do not think the Germans as a nation are any worse than the English or the Italians. We are all tarred with the same brush; we are all members of the vast human family. I decline to draw any distinctions . . . I cannot claim any superiority for India." He was merely opposed to aggressive governments. He therefore made a public pledge the day after war's beginning not to embarrass England; he in fact gave Britain and her allies his moral support. Further than this he would not go. He could not participate in the war effort.

The Congress party was not similarly inhibited. With the exception of Gandhi's close ashram disciples and men like Khan Abdul Ghaffar Khan, "the Frontier Gandhi," a gentle giant Pathan, few Congress leaders were pacifists or believed in nonviolence. They followed Gandhi in his nonviolent campaigns because that was usually the price they had to pay for his leadership and because India had no choice, she had no arms. Gandhi knew this. With him nonviolence was a creed, with Congress, he said, "a policy." Congress, therefore, was ready to bring India wholeheartedly into the war for a compensation: "A free democratic India," Congress affirmed in a manifesto drafted by Nehru, "will gladly associate herself with other free nations for mutual defence against aggression and for economic co-operation. . . ." "I would fight Japan sword in hand," Nehru said on a subsequent occasion, "but I can only do so as a free man." Gandhi did not interfere, he merely abstained.

But the British government had no intention of giving India freedom, independence, Dominion status, or even lesser rights. Winston Churchill was Prime Minister and he was always guided by his famous dictum of November 10, 1942, "I have not become the King's First Minister in order to preside at the liquidation of the British Empire." He detested, probably feared, the "half-naked fakir" who loved England but would destroy the Empire. "Gandhism and all it stands for must ultimately be grappled with and finally crushed," Churchill said in 1935. Now, for the first time since 1935, Churchill was in office, supreme office, and he intended to crush Gandhism in order to save his England.

A great man is all of one piece, like good sculpture. Churchill and Gandhi were alike in that each gave his life to a single cause. Churchill's absorbing purpose was the preservation of Britain as a first-class power. He was a product of the nineteenth century and loved it. He loved royalty, caste, empire. Lloyd George despised the British upper classes, the generals, the nobility, and fought them. Churchill wished to perpetuate them. His attachment was not so much to them as to the nineteenth century that made them. The nineteenth century was the British Century, the century of Pax Britannica after the defeat of Napoleonic France and before the rise of Kaiser Germany, the century of the flowering of empire under Queen Victoria. Britain's past glory was Winston's god. The upper classes were synonymous to him with the greatness of his country. So was parliamentary democracy, so was India.

Churchill fought the Second World War to preserve the heritage of Britain. Would he permit a half-naked fakir to rob her of that heritage? "We mean to hold our own," Churchill said. India was England's property. He refused to relinquish it. From the time he became the King's First Minister in 1940, to the day in 1945 when he was ousted from office, Churchill waged war with Mahatma Gandhi. It was a contest between the past of England and the future of India.

To Churchill power was poetry. He was a Byronic Napoleon. He passionately hated the foreign tyrannies which threatened England and directed against them all the moral fervor his genius could generate, but had no sympathy for Gandhi's moral struggle against British domination. He would have died to keep England free but detested those who wanted India free. To him, Indians were the pedestal of a throne.

This explains the failure of the mission undertaken by Sir Stafford Cripps on behalf of the British government in the middle of 1942. Cripps, the thin, austere, rich, ascetic, vegetarian Labourite, could have come to an agreement with the Congress party, indeed held it within his grasp, but Churchill had visions of Gandhi striding up the steps of the Viceroy's palace to share power with the King-Emperor and would have none of that.

In the historic perspective of subsequent events it is clear that 1942 would have been the best time to take Patel, Nehru, Rajagopalachari, Azad, and their colleagues up those steps, past the superbly handsome, statuesque, motionless, colorful Indian guards with their lances, into the inner chambers of power and thus prepare the way for an independent India voluntarily associated, as now, in the Commonwealth. The British army and police, then in full control, would have guaranteed a peaceful transition and obviated the vivisection of India into the Indian Republic and Pakistan with all the enormous expense in lives, hatreds, economic deterioration, and political tensions which both are paying and may continue to pay for decades. Some sensed this then. "We will be out of here two years after the war ends," Sir Reginald Maxwell, Home Member in the Viceroy's Council, said to me, with remarkable prevision, in 1942. "We are not going to remain in India," the Viceroy told me in an interview. Perhaps Churchill knew it too. But the same gloriously indomitable will which enabled Churchill to stand unflinching in the face of what seemed inevitable defeat at Hitler's hands made him an unyielding block on India's road to her inevitable freedom. He would not be the instrument of liquidating the Empire. That was left to another British government of another England, noble in victory but weakened by its price.

## 24   My Week with Gandhi

The tonga, a one-horse, two-wheel carriage in which the passengers face backward, took Gandhi's dentist and me from the town of Wardha to the village of Sevagram. During the dusty five-mile ride I tried to make him talk about the Mahatma as a patient. He talked about the British in India.

Gandhi awaited us where the road meets the village. It was the first time I had seen him. He stepped toward me with an outstretched arm and open hand saying, "Mr. Fischer." He appeared taller than I had thought. Wearing only his celebrated loincloth and sandals, he was a contrast in gleaming white and soft brown. He looked well-built, with barrel chest, thin waist, and long, thin, muscular legs and pronounced knee bulges. He was seventy-three. He beckoned me to a bench, sat down first, and with his palm stroked the place where I was to sit down. The way he did it suggested, "This is my house, come in." I immediately felt at home.

Sensing my desire to know what was in store for me, he said I could have an hour's talk with him after lunch and walk with him in the evening. He would put me in the care of Kurshed Naoroji, granddaughter of the famous

Parsi Indian nationalist Dadabhai Naoroji, who had given up her voice studies in Europe to serve Gandhi. She presently appeared and installed me in the mud-walled, bamboo-roofed guest hut which consisted of a room with an earthen floor and a small adjoining room with tubs, pails, and pitchers of water on its cement floor. It was 110 degrees outside and not much less inside and five or six splash baths per day were the minimum for comfort. The village and ashram had no running water, electricity, fans, radio, or telephone. It was India.

At eleven, Kurshed led me to Gandhi's hut. I left my slippers outside and stepped into a dim room where Gandhi lay on a pallet on the earthen floor. Beside him were some manuscripts and a wooden stand, ten inches high, with several circular holes in which stood his fountain pen and pencil. I was introduced to the secretaries: Mahadev Desai, Pyarelal, and Kishorlal Mashruwala. After a moment, Gandhi rose lithely and, in a tone of mock command said to me, "Come along." It was lunchtime. "Now put on your shoes and hat," he said. "Those are two indispensable things here. Don't get a sunstroke."

Two long walls of matting connected by a back wall and roof of the same material constituted the dining hall. Each person, about thirty in all including children, had a thin straw mat under him and a brass tray in front of him. Gandhi sat on a cushion. Male and female members of the ashram, moving noiselessly on bare feet, deposited food on the trays, and pots and pans at Gandhi's legs. He handed me a bronze bowl filled with vegetable mush in which I thought I discerned chopped spinach leaves and pieces of squash. A woman poured some salt on my tray, another gave me a metal tumbler with warm water and a second metal tumbler with warm milk. Then I got two little boiled potatoes in jackets and several soft, flat circular wheat-cakes. Gandhi—I was sitting one removed from him—handed me one hard, paper-thin wheatcake from a metal container in front of him.

At the sound of a gong, a robust young man in shorts stopped waiting on the trays, stood erect, closed his eyes so that only a white slit remained open—it made him look blind—and began a high-pitched chant in which all joined. The prayer ended with "Shahnti, Shahnti, Shahnti," Peace,

Peace, Peace. Everybody then began eating with their
fingers, fishing out the vegetable mush with a wheatcake
folded into a triangle. I was given a teaspoon. Gandhi
munched busily, stopping only to serve his wife and near
neighbors.

"You have lived in Soviet Russia for fourteen years.
What is your opinion of Stalin?" This was Gandhi's first
political remark to me.

I felt very hot, my hands were sticky, and my ankles
and legs had commenced to hurt from sitting on them, so
I replied briefly, "Very able and very ruthless."

"As ruthless as Hitler?" he asked.

"At least."

After a pause, he turned to me and said, "Have you
seen the Viceroy?" I said yes. ("Make no mistake about
it," the Viceroy had told me, "the old man is the biggest
thing in India.")

The waiters brought second helpings of the same foods.
"You can have all the water you want," Gandhi volunteered. "We take good care that it is boiled. And now eat
your mango." I began to peel it and he laughed and others
did too. He explained that they usually turned and squeezed
it in their hands to soften it and then sucked out the pulp
through one end, but he added that I had the right to peel
it to see whether it was good.

Dinner, with almost the same menu, was just before
sundown. I took breakfast alone in the guest hut: tea,
biscuits, bread, butter, honey, and mango. At lunch the
second day, Gandhi exchanged my teaspoon for a table-
spoon. "This is more commensurate with your size," he
bantered. He offered me a boiled onion. I preferred a raw
one, a relief from the flat diet. At lunch the third day,
Gandhi said, "Fischer, give me your bowl, I will fill it with
vegetables." I told him that after eating the same mess of
spinach and squash four times in two days I had no desire
for more.

"You don't like vegetables," he commented.

"I don't like the taste of these vegetables three days
running."

"Ah," he suggested, "you must add plenty of salt and
lemon."

"You want me to kill the taste."

"No," he laughed, "enrich the taste."

"You're so nonviolent, you wouldn't even kill a taste."

"If that were the only thing men killed, I wouldn't mind," he remarked.

I wiped the perspiration from my face and neck. "Next time I'm in India . . ." I began. He did not seem to be listening so I stopped.

"Yes," he urged, "next time you're in India . . ."

"You either ought to have air conditioning in Sevagram or live in the Viceroy's palace."

"All right," he agreed without indicating his choice.

He encouraged banter and fun. One afternoon he quoted a remark he had made in London to Lord Sankey. "Do you think," he had said, "that I would have reached this green old age if I didn't take care of myself? This is one of my faults."

"I thought you were perfect," I quipped.

He laughed and the eight or ten ashramites who usually sat in on the afternoon talks laughed too. (He had asked whether I objected to their presence.) "No," he affirmed, "I am very imperfect. Before you are gone you will discover a hundred of my faults, and if you don't, I will help you."

Usually the interview started with his finding me the coolest place on the floor. Then with a smile, he would say, "Now, I invite your blows." Once, after a Moslem woman had brought him a mud pack for his abdomen, he stretched out and said, "I will take your blows lying down." At the end of the hour, he would look at his dollar watch and announce, "Your hour is up." He was minutely punctual.

Once as I was leaving he said, "Go sit in a tub." I wondered whether this was the Indian equivalent of "go sit on a tack." But crossing the sun-baked hundred yards between his hut and the guest house, the heat dried the inside of my head and I decided that sitting in a tub would be an excellent idea. In fact I thought I could improve on it. After each talk I would type out the verbatim record, and this was the day's ordeal, for in five minutes I was tired and covered with sweat. Stimulated by Gandhi's suggestion to sit in a tub, I placed a small wooden packing case in one of the tin washtubs filled with water, put a folded Turkish towel on the case, and then set a taller packing case just outside the tub and placed my portable typewriter on it. Having completed these arrangements, I sat down, naked, on the box in the tub and typed my notes. At intervals of a few minutes, as soon as I began to perspire, I dipped a bronze bowl into the tub and poured the water over my neck, back, and legs. This method enabled me to type for a whole hour without feeling exhausted. The innovation stirred the ashram to mirth and jolly comment. It was not at all a glum community. Gandhi saw to that.

The nights were refreshing and relaxing. Everyone slept outside his or her hut on a rope net covered with a pallet and held up by four foot-high wooden supports. I slept better than I had for years. The nights were quiet and the skies full of stars. Kurshed cautioned me against stepping on the ground in the dark without shoes; there were scorpions about.

Mornings at five when I walked over to Gandhi's hut, I would find him sitting on his bed in the open air eating a breakfast of mango pulp with a spoon. The meager meal finished, he would accept a towel and a long, rectangular, narrow-necked, corked bottle of water from Kasturbai and wash his hands before starting on a stroll across nearby fields. Once a drop of yellow mango juice fell on his loincloth and he scratched the stain busily for several minutes. On the morning and evening walks he leaned his arms on the shoulders of two young boys or girls—they would vie each time for the pleasure—but moved forward with long strides and talked throughout the half hour without tiring or losing his breath.

His body did not give the impression of age. His skin was soft and smooth, and had a healthy glow. His beautiful hands did not shake when he ate or wrote. He never reminisced. Lloyd George in his seventies would commence to answer a question on current events and soon be talking about his conduct of a First World War campaign or his fight for social reform at the turn of the century. Gandhi concentrated on plans for the future and the struggles of the day. The vigor of his social thinking also attested to his intellectual youthfulness. He became less conservative as he grew older. In the nineteenth twenties and thirties, for instance, he advocated voluntary gifts of land by landlords to peasants, but a decade later, while not abandoning the voluntary method, he urged a more drastic policy. "The peasants would take the land," he said, when I inquired about his land program for a free India. I asked whether the landlords would be compensated. "No," he replied, "that would be fiscally impossible." Sclerosis had not damaged his capacity to change, to learn, and to act.

His face of course betrayed his age. It formed a small part of a high-domed head from which the big ears stuck out almost at right angles. The upper lip, covered with a black-and-white stubble mustache, was so narrow it nearly met the fat, down-pointed nose. The expression of his face came from the soft, quiet, gentle eyes, the sensitive lower lip which portrayed self-control, strength, and suffering, and the ever-present smile revealing naked gums. (He wore his dentures only for eating and after a meal took them out and washed them in public.) The facial features, with the exception of the eyes, were ugly, and in repose his face would have been ugly, but it was scarcely ever in repose. Whether he was speaking or listening or thinking it was a twinkling mirror with many facets which reflected what went on behind it. He did not attempt to formulate his ideas in finished form; he thought aloud so one could hear the brain tick. You heard not just words, you heard his thoughts being born. You did not receive a polished prop-aganda product as with most politicians; you watched a mental process which was creative for him and you.

Lloyd George looked the great man. Churchill and Franklin D. Roosevelt showed stature and distinction. Not Gandhi. Close informal proximity at talks, walks, and meals with this man four-fifths naked was least conducive to awe or veneration, yet for that very reason it brought out the miracle of his personality with a mighty impact. All the props of the big man's impressiveness—the palace or his-toric mansion, the guards, the wait in the antechamber, the closed door about to open, the power of the office—were lacking. Gandhi's on-the-earth simplicity, devoid of the appearances or reality of power, emphasized his authority. The omnipotent dictator is least likely to have any author-ity. Gandhi had no power to compel, punish, or reward. His power was nil, his authority enormous. It came of love. Living with him one could see why he was loved: he loved. Not merely in isolated incidents, but day in, and day out, morning, noon, and night, for decades, in every act and word, he had manifested his love of individuals and of mankind. Nor could one fail to notice, in each sentence and attitude, his lifelong loyalty to a few simple, widely flouted principles: the exaltation of means over ends; non-violence; the primacy of truth; the curing qualities of trust; and consideration for the other person's doubts, time-lag, environment, and inner conflicts. He faced each day's issues in the light of eternal and universal values. By going to the ethical heart of a practical problem and sloughing off superficial considerations he found the permanent nucleus in the ephemeral. It enabled him to split the social atom and find a new source of energy in the masses. Some had written and spoken as well as he or better. Gandhi's greatness lay in doing what others might do but don't. One sat in wonder before the miracle, for it apparently was an effortless way of life rather than a conscious program.

"Perhaps he will not succeed," Tagore wrote of Gandhi. "Perhaps he will fail as the Buddha failed and as Christ failed to wean men from their iniquities, but he will always be remembered as one who made his life a lesson for all ages to come." Gandhi had risen above his acts, he had gained considerable independence of their success or failure. It was he who was important, not his deeds or words. This may be why men could differ with his views without rejecting him, and accept his policies against their better judgment without feeling humiliated.

One evening I went to Mahadev Desai's hut and watched him spin. I said I had been listening to Gandhi and studying my notes and wondering what was the source of his hold on people; I had come to the tentative conclusion that it was his passion.

"That is right," he agreed.

"What is the root of his passion?" I asked.

"This passion is the sublimation of all the passions that flesh is heir to," he explained.

"Sex?"

"Sex and anger and personal ambition. Gandhi is under his own complete control. That generates tremendous energy and passion."

The week I spent in the ashram this energy and passion were driving Gandhi toward another campaign of civil disobedience. Sir Stafford Cripps had come and failed and gone; Churchill opposed Indian independence. Ever eager, like Krishna, to be in action, the Mahatma, in June, 1942, was contemplating an antigovernment movement under the slogan "Quit India." Action was his antidote to frustration.

Gandhi held that the position of the democracies in the war was morally indefensible if India did not gain her independence. "Your President," he said to me one afternoon, "talks about the Four Freedoms. Do they include the freedom to be free?" Roosevelt had actually pressed Churchill to yield and allow Cripps to win the Indians for the war effort, but the King's First Minister remained adamant.

Jawaharlal Nehru and Maulana Azad, the Congress President, nevertheless opposed Gandhi's proposed civil disobedience campaign. Nehru spent three days arguing with Gandhi in the ashram while I was there. "He fought my position with a passion which I have no words to describe," Gandhi reported affectionately in *Harijan*. Nehru's personal contacts, he explained, "make him feel much more the misery of the impending ruin of China and Russia. . . . In that misery he tried to forget his old quarrel with [British] imperialism. But before he left the ashram the logic of facts," as Gandhi put it, "overwhelmed him." More likely Gandhi overwhelmed him. In my presence Gandhi told Nehru that he would launch civil disobedience whether he joined or not.

Something deep in Nehru's nature rebels against surrender. The automatic obedience most Indians gave Gandhi repelled Jawaharlal. He acquired a feeling of independence from saying No to the unquestioned master; resistance lent him the illusion of strength. His public outbursts of temper and his oratorical thunderbolts of defiance were likewise psychological reinforcements for a person who needed them. In this respect he was strangely like India and unlike Gandhi. Nehru played at strength. A weak person and weak nation made the motions and sounds of the strong. The strong Gandhi lent strength to the weak.

But having been overwhelmed by the Mahatma's urgency, Nehru became a more unbending advocate of the civil disobedience campaign than Gandhi himself. Gandhi was malleable. "It seems to me," I argued in the course of an afternoon interview, "that the British cannot possibly quit India altogether. That would mean making a present of India to Japan. England would never agree, nor would the United States approve. If you demand that the British pack up bag and baggage, you are simply asking the impossible; you are barking up a tree. You do not mean, do you, that they must also withdraw their armies?"

For at least two minutes a heavy silence filled the hut. Gandhi had listened and was now listening to himself. "You are right," he said finally. "No, Britain and America and other countries too can keep their armies here and use India as a base for military operations." Later that day Mashruwala told me he vehemently dissented from this view. But Gandhi was ready to compromise and he wrote President Roosevelt that "if the Allies think it necessary they may keep their troops, at their own expense, in India. . . ." "Tell your President I wish to be dissuaded," he said to me. He was prepared to cancel his plans for civil disobedience and wanted to discuss the matter with the Viceroy. Before I left the ashram Desai told me to suggest to the Viceroy a meeting with Gandhi. I was not at liberty to disclose this to Nehru but when, en route to Delhi, I met him in the Bombay home of his sister, Mrs. Krishna Hutheesing, I asked whether he thought Gandhi ought to see the Viceroy. "No, what for?" Nehru exclaimed. He was again resisting surrender, whereas Gandhi still hoped he and Linlithgow could find the road to a settlement. Uncompromising on principles, Gandhi would always compromise on time and pace.

Lord Linlithgow refused to see Gandhi.

## 25   Frustration and Irritation

In May, June, and July, 1942, one felt a suffocating airlessness in India. The Japanese aggressors were next door, in Burma. England seemed too weak to protect India from invasion. Vocal political Indians were exasperated by their utter helplessness. They could neither defend their country nor exploit Britain's emergency to free it.

In this ugly mood, the All-India Congress Committee

met in Bombay on August 7th, to debate Gandhi's proposed civil disobedience campaign. Conciliatory despite rebuffs, the Mahatma told A. T. Steele of the New York *Herald Tribune* that "if anybody could convince me that in the midst of war the British government cannot declare India free without jeopardizing the war effort, I should like to hear the argument."

Would he desist from civil disobedience if he were convinced? Steele asked.

"Of course," Gandhi replied. "My complaint is that these good people talk *at* me, swear *at* me, but never condescend to talk *to* me."

Shortly after midnight of August 8th, Gandhi addressed the delegates. A resolution approving the civil disobedience movement had been passed. But he warned them that "the actual struggle does not commence this very moment." As on similar occasions in previous years, he recalled, "You have merely placed certain powers in my hands." He would try to avert trouble. "My first act will be to wait upon His Excellency the Viceroy. . . ." Two or three weeks might pass. What were they to do in the meanwhile? "There is the spinning wheel. . . . But there is something more you have to do. . . . Every one of you should, from this very moment, consider himself a free man or woman and even act as if you are free and no longer under the heel of imperialism." This reversed the materialistic concept that conditions determine psychology. No, Gandhi was saying, man can remake his psychology and thereby his condition. "What you think you become," he once stated.

Obviously, Gandhi, knowing the temper of the country, saw the necessity for action. Obviously, he feared violent action and, to prevent it, planned another attempt at an understanding with the Viceroy. Obviously, the Viceroy was under instructions not to parley with the half-naked rebel. Before sunrise on the 9th, Gandhi, Nehru, and scores of other top-rank Congressmen were carried off to prison. Gandhi, with Mrs. Naidu, Mahadev Desai, Miss Slade, and Pyarelal, was quartered in the Aga Khan's palace at Yeravda, near Poona. The next day, Kasturbai and Dr. Sushila Nayyar were brought in.

The moment the prison doors closed behind Gandhi the sluice gates of violence opened. Police stations and government buildings were set on fire, railroad ties pulled up, telegraph lines destroyed, and British officials assaulted and killed. A powerful underground movement sprang into existence led, in most cases, by the Socialists who were then a segment of Congress. In some areas His Majesty's writ no longer ran; free-Indian governments were established in a number of towns and districts.

British declarations laid the blame for the turbulence at Gandhi's door. In a letter from prison to the Viceroy Gandhi repelled the charge and accused the government of "distortions and misrepresentations."

The Viceroy's reply dissented.

That he, the apostle of nonviolence, should be called the author of widespread, bloody violence, apparently irritated Gandhi out of his equanimity. On New Year's Eve, 1942, he wrote the Viceroy again. "This is a very personal letter. . . . I must not allow the old year to expire without disburdening myself of what is rankling in my breast against you. I have thought we were friends. . . . Why did you not, before taking drastic action, send for me? . . . I am quite capable of seeing myself as others see me." The government "wronged innocent men." It, not he, had provoked the arson and murders, but since it insisted on accusing him falsely he would fast, "crucify the flesh by fasting."

A return letter from the Viceroy stigmatized the contemplated fast as "political blackmail." Nevertheless, two days before the scheduled beginning of the fast the government offered to release Gandhi and all his colleagues. He refused. He was not fasting to win a release; the fast "is on my part an appeal to the Highest Tribunal for justice which I have failed to secure from you." He was innocent and wished to purge himself of the reproach.

The three-week fast almost killed him. On the thirteenth day, Kasturbai knelt before a sacred plant and prayed; she had given him up for lost. His pulse was feeble and his skin cold. He survived.

Gandhi found no rest. He sought "soothing balm for my pain." He bombarded officials and nonofficials in India and England with evidence that he bore no responsibility for the destruction and deaths caused by the underground and its repression. If he had been a free man he might have

prevented the violence, he might have fasted against his
fellow Congressmen involved in the turmoil. None of his
letters was published at the time. He had no access to the
press. He could neither publicly rebut the false arguments
of the government nor check the violence of his friends.
A tempestuous resentment raged within his breast. He
underwent torments. A perfect yogi would have remained
indifferent, but the Mahatma was not completely detached.

To compound the tragedy, Mahadev Desai, Gandhi's
friend, adviser, and chronicler, whom he treasured more
than a son, died by his side in prison of a heart attack.
And on February 22, 1944, Kasturbai, her head resting in
her husband's lap, breathed her last. The Mahatma was
disconsolate. In this too he had not achieved detachment.
He mourned the dead. Thereafter, on the 22nd of every
month until he died, Gandhi conducted a memorial service
for Kasturbai at which prayers were sung and the entire
text of the *Gita* recited.

Six weeks after his wife's passing, Gandhi suffered a
severe attack of benign tertian malaria which made him
delirious. Agitation for his release swept India. Death was
expected momentarily. The government placed a heavy
armed guard around the prison. At 8 A.M. on May 6, 1944,
Gandhi and his associates were released. This was his last
time in jail. Altogether, he spent 2,089 days in Indian jails
(almost six years) and 249 days in South African prisons.

He recuperated at the beach near Bombay in the pleasant home of a friend. The hostess suggested that he ought
to see a moving picture; he had never seen a silent movie
or talkie. He agreed reluctantly. *Mission to Moscow,* on
view in an adjacent suburb, was brought to the house and
demonstrated.

How did he like it?

"I didn't like it," he declared. He hadn't liked the ball-
room dancing with the scantily-clad women.

He spent several weeks relaxing and gaining strength.

## 26   Jinnah Versus Gandhi

Having walked back into the political arena in June, 1944,
Gandhi tried to get an appointment with the new Viceroy,

Lord Wavell, a gentleman, general, and poet. Wavell refused to see him. Spurred by Rajagopalachari, who in some ways out-Gandhied Gandhi as a conciliator, the Mahatma now wrote Mohammed Ali Jinnah, president of the Moslem League, suggesting talks. Congress-League agreement, Gandhi felt, would impel the British in India to yield power. "Brother Jinnah," was Gandhi's salutation to the Moslem chief, and he signed himself "Your brother, Gandhi." Jinnah's reply was addressed to "Dear Mr. Gandhi," and signed "M. A. Jinnah." In subsequent correspondence, Gandhi began his letters with "Dear Quaid-e-Azam," or Great Leader, a recently-assumed title. Jinnah still wrote "Dear Mr. Gandhi." Their conversations lasted seventeen days and ended in zero.

In May, 1945, Germany surrendered. On July 26, 1945, the Labour party decisively defeated the Conservatives and Clement R. Attlee replaced Churchill as Prime Minister. On August 14, 1945, Japan surrendered. The new Labour government immediately announced that it sought "an early realization of self-government in India" and summoned Wavell to Whitehall. On the Viceroy's return to Delhi he promised the restoration of provincial rule by Indians, and an assembly to draft a federal constitution. He also would form a Congress-Moslem Executive Council, a sort of Cabinet under British supervision, in the federal capital. But Jinnah would accept only the partition of India. "We could settle the Indian problem in ten minutes," he declared in Bombay in December, 1945, "if Mr. Gandhi would say, 'I agree that there should be Pakistan: I agree that one-fourth of India, composed of six provinces—Sind, Baluchistan, the Punjab, the Northwest Frontier Province, Bengal, and Assam—with their present boundaries, constitute the Pakistan state.' "

Mr. Gandhi, however, could not say it. He regarded the "vivisection" of India as "blasphemy." In any case, the bisection of India on Jinnah's terms was impossible and unjust. He wanted Pakistan so that Hindus would not rule over Moslems. But Assam, which he demanded for Pakistan, had only 3,442,479 Moslems as against 6,762,254 non-Moslems. In the vast Punjab province, the Moslems numbered 16,217,242; non-Moslems 12,201,577. In Bengal, with about sixty million inhabitants, Moslems constituted 52 per cent, little more than half. In these three regions alone, if they were included in Pakistan, fifty million Moslems would rule over forty-seven million Hindus and Sikhs. Pakistan would be born with a leaden minority problem around its infant neck. At the same time, Jinnah's proposed Pakistan left twenty million Moslems, or one-fifth of India's Moslems, under Hindu rule. Yet Jinnah was deaf to logic and blind to arithmetic. Irrational resoluteness, even when it conflicts with self-interest, nevertheless often makes history.

Mohammed Ali Jinnah was a remarkable figure. Over six feet tall, he weighed 120 pounds and was a very thin man. Thick, long silver-gray hair, brushed straight back, covered his well-shaped head. The shaven face was thin, the nose long and aquiline. His temples and cheeks were deep holes which made the cheekbones stand out like high horizontal ridges. When he was not speaking, he would pull in his chin, tighten his lips, and knit his brow into an expression of forbidding earnestness. He almost never laughed. He frequently wore European clothes, but for public appearances, and some private ones too, he wore a Moslem costume: a knee-length straw-colored tunic, tight white Indian trousers that clung to his bony legs, black patent-leather pumps—and a monocle on a black cord. He was "undoubtedly," wrote George E. Jones in the *New York Times* of May 5, 1946, "one of the best dressed men in the British Empire." Mr. Jones, who interviewed Jinnah several times, described Jinnah in his book, *Tumult in India,* as "a superb political craftsman, a Machiavelli in the amoral sense of that description. . . . His personal defects are a somewhat hostile reserve, conceit, and a narrow outlook. . . . He is an extremely suspicious man, who feels that he has been wronged many times in life. His repressed intensity borders on the psychotic. Withdrawn, and isolated, Jinnah is arrogant to the point of discourtesy. . . ."

Jinnah was not a devout Moslem. He infringed the Islamic code by drinking alcohol, eating pork, and seldom going to mosque. He knew little Urdu and no Arabic. He went outside his religious community—in his forties—to marry a Parsi girl of eighteen. Yet the irreligious Jinnah wanted two religious states, while the religious Gandhi would countenance only a united secular state.

Jinnah, the first child of a rich merchant of skins, hides and gum arabic, was a Khoja Moslem. The Khojas were recent converts to Islam. Many Khojas maintain the Hindu joint family system and carry Hindu names; "Jinnah" is a Hindu name. In the eighteenth and nineteenth centuries, the Khojas attempted to return to Hinduism but were repeatedly rebuffed. This may have been an unconscious factor in Jinnah's hatred of Hindus.

It was personal too. "I have been in this movement for thirty-five years," he said to me in the first of two interviews in his opulent Bombay villa in June, 1942. "Nehru worked under me in the Home Rule Society. Gandhi worked under me. I was active in the Congress party. . . . My goal was Hindu-Moslem unity. . . . So it was until 1920 when Gandhi came into the limelight. A deterioration of Hindu-Moslem relations set in. . . . I had the distinct feeling that unity was hopeless, that Gandhi did not want it. I was a disappointed man. I decided to stay in England. I did not even go back to India to sell my possessions but sold them through an agent. I remained in England until 1935. I took up law practice before the Privy Council, and contrary to my expectations, I was a success."

In an article on Jinnah in the London *Economist* of September 17, 1949, an author who obviously knew his subject reported that while Jinnah was practicing law in London, somebody "repeated to him that Nehru, whom he despised and hated, had imprudently said at a private party that 'Jinnah was finished.' Outraged, Jinnah packed up and sailed back to India at once just to 'show Nehru.' . . . To Cleopatra's nose as factor in history one should perhaps add Jinnah's pride."

Hurt pride is a ferocious beast. Jealousy aroused by the bottom view of a rival mounting the ladder can become a mighty urge to achieve power in order to hurt him and others. Such motivations have made history. But history must help by offering the jealous one an opportunity, it must cup its hands under his foot to give him a boost. Historic events did form a stirrup for Jinnah's climb into the saddle. The upper- and middle-class Moslems of India were indeed fearful of Hindu rule, and as Gandhi's work in the 1920's and 1930's made independence inevitable in the foreseeable future they organized to thwart it. A free India, they believed, would be a Hindu-dominated India, "Hindu-raj" they called it, and it is true that one hundred million Moslems would always be a minority among three hundred million non-Moslems (Hindus, Sikhs, Parsis, Christians, and others) if religious sentiments shaped politics. Rich Moslems and the emerging Mohammedan middle class of intellectuals and merchants assumed that in a Hindu-majority free India Hindus would get most of the government posts and enjoy other economic advantages. They were therefore reluctant to see the departure of the British who helped them obtain political jobs and adequate political representation.

The envisaged Pakistan, however, would give Moslems all the political power and jobs and control over all industry and trade. Even more important was the peasantry. With the exception of Jinnah, the founders and bosses of the Moslem League were landlords who expected a Nehru-led India to parcel out their estates among the cultivators. The Congress party of the purely-Moslem Northwest Frontier Province had actually won political power by organizing the peasants. But a theocratic Pakistan, the upper class hoped, would be poison to social radicalism; the peasant, presumably, could be persuaded to put country above land.

Pakistan was thus the answer to the rich Moslem's prayers and middle-class Moslem's dreams. A religious state offered them social safety and a political and economic monopoly.

No one motivated by sordid landlord gains or the clerk's ambitions of the educated unemployed or the obscurantism of the mullahs (preachers) could have fused all these urges into a national crusade. That required somebody who stood above them, as Hitler personally stood above the financial and business aims of the German upper bourgeoisie and East Prussian land barons. Jinnah was the man. Incorruptible, rich and disinterested in economic benefits for himself, his furious hatred of Gandhi and Nehru, who had "worked under" him and driven him out of politics, plus his conceit and "repressed intensity" bordering on the psychotic brought him back to politics in his sixties with a zeal that knew no principle except success. Interviewing Jinnah was like listening to a cracked phonograph record, no argument, merely endless repetition of slogans: Hindus and Moslems Are Separate Nations; Gandhi Wants Hindu-Raj; Pakistan Must Be. This single-minded fanaticism, unreasoning passion, and unbounded hate wrapped in a person untouched by suspicions of selfish motives had an enormous appeal to people whose hard lives and frustrations made them an easy prey to simple goals charged with emotion: Moslems will have their own state; Moslems will rule Hindus and Sikhs instead of being ruled; the Hindu merchant, industrialist, landlord, and official will go. The victims of Jinnah were as oblivious as he to the mathematics of minorities and to practical considerations. He gave them an intoxicating banner: Pakistan. He thought only of achieving Pakistan, never of the problems of Pakistan. In fact for the first few years after he broached the idea he even refused to indicate the future borders of Pakistan. The less concrete the project the more fascinating and the less attainable by criticism. The situation was a fanatic's paradise.

Jinnah had become Gandhi's biggest problem.

# PART THREE
# Victory and Tragedy

*March 24, 1946—January 30, 1948*

## 27  Seeking the Divine in Man

Gandhi had decided that he wanted to live to be a hundred and twenty-five years old, not, of course, as "an animated corpse, a burden to one's relatives and society," but physically fit and active. Everybody can attain such a ripe age, he contended, by means of nature cure: no medicines, just right diet, mud packs, baths, regular sleep, internal irrigation when necessary, no alcohol, no stimulants—provided one also possessed the real key to longevity: "detachment of mind." The "nectar" which sustains life is service and renunciation of fruits. That leaves "no room for worry or impatience." Unselfishness preserves life, whereas love of the ego kills it. In a way Gandhi's yearning to survive for another half century was a conceit as well as a reflection of his faith and realism. The work that remained to be done could be done, but not in mortal man's normal span.

When I visited Mahatma Gandhi again at the end of June, 1946, he was in fine fettle. I had no sooner arrived in New Delhi than I taxied to the untouchables' slum where he lived. The evening devotional meeting was in progress and I posted myself at the foot of the three wooden steps where Gandhi would descend from the prayer platform. "Ah, there you are," he said; "well, I have not grown better-looking in these four years."

"I would not dare differ with you," I replied. He threw back his head and laughed. Taking me by the elbow, he strolled toward his stone hut, inquired about my health, trip, and family, and then asked me to walk with him at

5:30 the next morning. In the following three weeks I
stayed with him for eight days in various parts of India.
His health was excellent. His hands shook slightly when
he ate and he did not stride as lustily as he had four years
earlier nor was his voice as strong, but he was quick in his
movements and regular in exercise. After dinner one day
at Dr. Dinshah Mehta's nature-cure clinic in Poona he
invited me to walk with him. "Surely you are not going to
walk in the rain," I protested lightly.

"Come along, old man," he said and stretched out an
arm. His love of fun and laughter was undimmed.

Nevertheless, shadows were darkening his life. "I have
not convinced India," he said to me. "There is violence all
around us. I am a spent bullet." He still thought he could
win the battle with his own people, and wanted more years
of health in which to do so, but his optimism, as intrinsic
as his muscles and bones, was now tinged with doubt.

In one respect, however, the most important, he remained the same: he was the karma yogi, the man who was
ever active, ever moving on and on toward the goal. The
least he could do was to do the most he could do. He
worked unceasingly with the numerous organizations he
had established for Harijan welfare, education, spinning,
and village uplift, and now started a foundation for nature
cure; he wrote several pieces every week for his English-
language and Gujarati-language papers; he answered
dozens of letters every day; and he collected money in
masses at meetings and from individuals, mostly from
wealthy friends. It was his money-milking of the rich which
evoked Mrs. Naidu's famous quip, "It costs a lot of money
to keep Gandhi poor." One textile millionaire, G. D. Birla,
supported the ashram, with its hospital and dairy, after
1935 at a cost of approximately $17,000 a year.

In addition to his manifold welfare activities, Gandhi
also gave his energy to the Congress party. Although the
strong man of Congress was Sardar Vallabhbhai Patel, and
its statesman, whether he agreed with its policy or, as frequently happened, did not, was C. Rajagopalachari, known
by most as Rajaji, Jawaharlal Nehru had actually been
designated Gandhi's political successor. Nehru was a low-
per cent Gandhian and no Gandhi, but between Gandhi and
Nehru a loving father-son relationship existed which no

disagreement could cool. "Somebody suggested that Pandit Jawaharlal and I were estranged," the Mahatma stated at a Congress executive meeting on January 15, 1942. "It will require much more than differences of opinion to estrange us. We have had differences from the moment we were co-workers, and yet I have said for some years past and say now that not Rajaji but Jawaharlal will be my successor. He says he does not understand my language, and that he speaks a language foreign to me. This may or may not be true. But language is no bar to the union of hearts. And I know this, that when I am gone he will speak my language."

"Nehru has an oratorical mind," Gandhi said to me in 1946. Patel boasted of being Gandhi's "Yes-man," Nehru was Gandhi's "No-Yes man." Hence Gandhi's hope that he would some day speak the Mahatma's heart language.

As national freedom drew near, political activities grew more intense and Gandhi stood at their epicenter. Nehru, Patel, Rajaji, and other leaders were daily visitors in the untouchables' slum. They came to win the approval without which they could never be sure of public acceptance of their plans and proposals; they came, equally, for Gandhi's guidance. They needed his "instinct," or intuition, a vague term which nevertheless became a central issue in the negotiations for the liberation of India.

An impressive British Cabinet Mission had arrived in India on March 23, 1946, to settle the terms of India's national liberation. Its members, Lord Pethick-Lawrence, the Secretary of State for India, Sir Stafford Cripps, President of the Board of Trade, and Albert V. Alexander, First Lord of the Admiralty, asked suggestions from Indian leaders on the arrangements needed to substitute Indian freedom for British rule. But the leaders of Congress and the Moslem League could not agree on what they wanted, and the Cabinet Mission therefore drafted its own plan and published it on May 16, 1946. After minute study, Gandhi stated his "conviction . . . that it is the best document the British government could have produced in the circumstances." England's "one purpose," he affirmed, "is to end British rule as early as may be."

The Cabinet Mission's announcement referred to "voluminous evidence" of an "almost universal desire, outside

the supporters of the Moslem League, for the unity of
India." On the other hand, it discovered a "very genuine
and acute anxiety" among Moslems "lest they should find
themselves subjected to a perpetual Hindu-Majority rule."
The Mission accordingly examined "closely and impartially
the possibility of a partition of India," but decided against
it. The "two halves of the proposed Pakistan state," the
Mission's declaration affirmed, "are separated by some
seven hundred miles, and the communications between
them both in war and peace would be dependent on the
good will of Hindustan." In the western half of Pakistan, it
pointed out, the non-Moslem minority would be 37 per
cent of the whole population, and in the eastern 48 per
cent, while twenty million Moslems would remain outside
Pakistan as a minority in Hindustan. "These figures show,"
the Mission document asserted, "that the setting up of a
separate sovereign state of Pakistan on the lines claimed by
the Moslem League would not solve the communal minority problem"—which was Pakistan's presumed purpose.

The three British Cabinet ministers then studied the wisdom of a lesser Pakistan, exclusive of Hindu and Sikh
areas, but "such a Pakistan," they said, "is regarded by the
Moslem League as quite impracticable." (Yet this is the
Pakistan which now exists.) The smaller Pakistan, the Ministers wrote, would necessitate the partitioning of Assam,
Bengal, and the Punjab, a measure which, in their opinion,
"would be contrary to the wishes of a very large percentage
of these provinces. Bengal and the Punjab," they continued, "each has its own common language and a long history
and tradition. Moreover, any division of the Punjab would
of necessity divide the Sikhs leaving substantial bodies of
Sikhs on both sides of the boundary."

For these reasons, the Cabinet Mission advised the British government not to divide India. It recommended, instead (1) a united India, embracing the British India and
the native states of the maharajas and rajas, with one federal government responsible for defense, foreign affairs,
and communications; (2) a federal parliament which could
pass no major measure of a racial or religious character unless a majority of the Hindu and of the Moslem deputies
voted for it; and (3) provincial governments with wide
powers. The federal government, checked by adequate safe-

guards for minorities, would be limited to a few, inescap-
ably national, tasks, while everything else was left to provincial governments which, in the areas with Moslem
majorities, would consist chiefly of Moslems.

The Constituent Assembly, called on to draft a constitution based on these principles, would meet briefly in New
Delhi and then break up into three sections. Section A
would comprise delegates from the Hindu-majority group
of provinces in central India; Section B delegates from the
heavily-Moslem provinces of western India embracing the
Northwest Frontier Province, Sind, and the Punjab; Section
C delegates from Bengal and Assam. The aim of these three
sectional constituent assemblies would be to frame constitutions for the three subfederations into which India was to
be divided.

It was on this rock that the British Mission's plan foun-
dered. Gandhi's instinct, as he called it, rebelled against the
sectional constituent assemblies. Maybe, he argued, the
Northwest Frontier province, which had always been pro-
Congress, would prefer to be part of Group A; why should
it be forced into group B? Assam was largely Hindu; why
should it go with Bengal which had a small Moslem majority? He considered that coercion. No, the British replied,
these areas would merely participate in the constitution-
writing assemblies and if later they did not like the constitutions they could withdraw and join another group. Thus
Assam could join Hindu Group A. Gandhi feared that it
would be too late after the constitution was drafted, that
Assam, for instance, or the Northwest Frontier province,
would be bound in some legal way and could not withdraw.
The fact is Gandhi, for once in his life and at a most critical
moment, was the victim of his own suspicions. He had
given the British a certificate of good will. On the other
hand, he entertained doubts: were these sections and
groups a ruse to slip in a quarter-Pakistan or half-Pakistan
by the back door?

The position was not made easier when Jinnah, after de-
nouncing the Cabinet Mission for using "commonplace and
exploded arguments" against Pakistan, nevertheless, on
June 4, accepted the Mission's plan. This may have been
shrewd politics and smart psychology, for anything the
Moslem League approved was *ipso facto* wrong to many

Congressmen. Congress debated the issue for weeks. Suspicions troubled them. Nehru, sitting cross-legged on my bed in Dr. Mehta's nature-cure clinic, and weighing British intentions, said, "It does not appear that they are getting ready to leave India." His constant companion, Mr. Krishna Menon, later High Commissioner in London and Indian delegate to the United Nations, shared and fed this skepticism. It was widespread in Congress ranks. In several months in India during that period I met almost no Indian nationalist who could persuade himself that England would part with power. It seemed unreal, too good to be true, too unnecessary. Some Congressmen, especially among the Socialists, who had enjoyed their baptism of violence in 1942 and 1943, thought independence would only be solid and permanent if they fought for it and expelled the British. As always, the political climate of the country seeped like a fog into the closed sessions of the politicians and influenced their decisions.

Gandhi's misgivings thickened the fog. Yet he did not allow Congress to reject the British plan; on the contrary, he insisted on its adoption. He said that since his reason did not support his instinct his suspicions might be unjustified. Congress accordingly agreed to participate in the Constituent Assembly. But the Mahatma's doubts survived in other minds, and early in July Nehru indicated at a lively Bombay press conference that Congress would not enter the sectional assemblies to draft constitutions for the three subfederations. This killed the British Mission's plan of May 16, 1946; Jinnah was now free to cancel his acceptance of the scheme.

In retrospect it seems that the British proposal was the best Gandhi, Nehru and Congress could have expected, better far than the partitioning of India which actually took place. To be sure, it can be argued that the Plan would not have worked, or that it would have led to full Pakistan anyway. But in politics it is never possible to prove that something that did not happen would have happened. The point is simply that the British plan of May, 1946—which might have been amended and improved—did provide for a united India with one federal government, and therefore might have prevented the horror of the subsequent bisecting surgery.

Whether Jinnah would have permitted a federal government of a united India to operate appears questionable. Viceroy Wavell had been trying to give birth to a provisional federal government representing Congress and the Moslem League. Jinnah agreed on condition, however, that he appoint all the Moslems in the Cabinet. Congress balked, for it had never considered itself purely Hindu, or religious; it had Moslem members, some of them, like President Azad, quite prominent. To have conceded Jinnah's sole right to select the Moslems in the government would have been to accept the proposition that the Moslem League spoke for all the Moslems of India, and that India, therefore, should be divided politically because it was divided religiously.

Faced with this cogent Congress objection, Wavell yielded to it and asked both organizations to submit their lists of candidates for the government on the understanding that no side could veto the nominees of the other. Thereupon Jinnah declined to participate in the government. On August 12, 1946, Wavell accordingly authorized Nehru to form the government. Nehru went to see Jinnah and offered him a choice of places in the Cabinet; Gandhi said Jinnah could even be Prime Minister or Defense Minister. Jinnah rejected the offer. Nehru then appointed a Cabinet consisting of six Congressmen, of whom five were caste Hindus and one a Harijan, as well as two Moslems, one Sikh, one Christian, and one Parsi.

Jinnah answered by declaring August 16th "Direct Action Day." A four-day riot took place in Calcutta in which, Lord Pethick-Lawrence stated, the casualties numbered "some five thousand dead and fifteen thousand wounded." Several days later one of the Moslems appointed to the Cabinet by Nehru was waylaid in a lonely spot in Simla and stabbed seven times. "Obviously political," high British authorities called the assault.

Nehru became Prime Minister of India on September 2nd. Jinnah proclaimed it a day of mourning and instructed Moslems to display black flags; the next day in Bombay, he said, "The Russians may have more than a spectator's interest in Indian affairs, and they are not very far from India either." He must have been very bitter and ready to invoke any means to attain his ends. The Moslem black flags were like red flags to a Hindu. Shootings and knifings occurred in Bombay and spread to the Punjab, Bihar, and Bengal. The Moslem League now announced that it would boycott the Constituent Assembly which it had agreed to support.

Gandhi said the country was nearing a state of civil war. Alarmed, Wavell redoubled his efforts to bring the Jinnahites into Nehru's government. Jinnah finally agreed and appointed five Cabinet ministers, four Moslems and one anti-Gandhi untouchable. Jinnah had always maintained that the Moslem League represented all Moslems and only Moslems. Why then should he have selected a Hindu, an untouchable, if not to annoy Congress and the caste Hindus? This indeed was Jinnah's purpose, and Liaquat Ali Khan, the foremost of the League members of the government, frankly stated that they did not recognize Nehru's government as the government of India and felt under no obligation to co-operate with it. Nor did they. They joined to sabotage it. The government was a house divided—by religion.

Most Congress members of the Cabinet and many of their assistants came to Gandhi's hut in the slums for advice; some came daily. He was "super-Prime Minister." He, however, kept his eye on the central issue: Hindu-Moslem relations. "I would rather that Hindus died without retaliation," he said of the continuing killings. Nor did the poisoned political situation divert his attention from other fundamental problems; he protested that when there was an epidemic, Harijans "are beaten and cannot draw water from the wells"; he urged the repeal of the Salt Tax, at the same time begging the people to be patient with new ministers laboring under unaccustomed burdens. He wrote on leprosy (he once massaged a leper who arrived at the ashram asking for help), and on the need of collective prayer.

The "raging fire" of Hindu-Moslem antagonism tormented him. "Why could I not suffer this anguish with unruffled calmness of spirit?" he asked. "I am afraid I have not the detachment required for living 125 years." Yet his faith in human beings persisted and found refreshing sustenance even in small crumbs. "In Bombay," he wrote in his magazine, "a Hindu gave shelter to a Moslem friend the other day. This infuriated the Hindu mob who demanded the head of the Moslem friend. The Hindu would not surrender his friend. So both went down, literally in deadly embrace. . . . Nor is this the first instance of chivalry in the midst of frenzy. During the recent blood bath in Calcutta, stories of Moslems having, at the peril of their lives, sheltered their Hindu friends and *vice versa* were recorded." He was encouraged. "Mankind," he said, "would die if there were no exhibition any time and anywhere of the divine in man."

From now till his death, Gandhi searched for the divine in man and the sane in India. Reports reached him of violence in the remote Noakhali and Tippera regions of East Bengal where Moslems were killing and forcibly converting Hindu men and ravishing Hindu women. That the turmoil was seeping into the villages disturbed Gandhi especially and he resolved to go to Noakhali. Friends tried to dissuade him; they said his health was bad and that the Congress members of the government needed him in New Delhi. "All I know is that I won't be at peace with myself unless I go there," he replied. He told people not to come to the railway station for his blessing, he was in no mood to give it. They came in hordes. En route to Bengal, immense crowds besieged the stations and overflowed onto the tracks. They climbed to the roofs of the terminals, broke windows and shutters and created an ear-splitting din. Several times the conductor gave the signal for the train's departure but someone pulled the emergency cord and the train stopped with a jerk. At one station the railway authorities turned the fire hose on the people on the track and flooded Gandhi's compartment. He arrived in Calcutta five hours late, tired from the noise and sad.

Thirty-two people had been killed in religious riots in Calcutta a few days before the Mahatma's arrival. With Mr. H. S. Suhrawardy, the Moslem Prime Minister of Bengal, Gandhi toured the affected areas of the city, driving through deserted streets piled two feet high with uncollected garbage and lined with gutted houses and closed shops. Gandhi said he was overcome by "a sinking feeling at the mass madness that can turn man into less than a brute." Yet his determination persisted. He would remain in Calcutta and Noakhali. "I am not going to leave Bengal," he told a prayer meeting, "until the last embers of the trouble are stamped out. I may stay on here for a whole year or more.

If necessary, I will die here. But I will not acquiesce in failure. If the only effect of my presence in the flesh is to make people look up to me in hope and expectation which I can do nothing to vindicate, it would be far better that my eyes are closed in death."

## 28  On the Eve

While preparing to go to Noakhali for what became one of the most astonishing chapters of his whole astonishing life, news came to Gandhi in Calcutta of black events in the neighboring province of Bihar, with a population of 31,-000,000 Hindus and 5,000,000 Moslems. Moslem attacks on Hindus in Noakhali had inflamed the Bihari Hindus. October 25th was declared "Noakhali Day." Speeches by Congressmen, who would probably have thrown themselves flat on the ground and kissed the Mahatma's toes, and sensational newspaper headlines exaggerating the number of Hindu victims in Noakhali, whipped the Hindus into hysteria, and thousands paraded through streets and country lanes shouting "Blood for Blood." In the following week, according to the Delhi correspondent of the London *Times,* "the number of persons officials verified as killed by rioters" in Bihar was 4,580. Gandhi later put the total at more than ten thousand, most of them Moslems. Given the low-boiling-point passions and the crowded conditions of India, massacres were usually on a mass scale.

Bowed with grief, Gandhi addressed a manifesto to the Biharis. "The misdeeds of the Bihari Hindus," he said, "may justify Qaid-e-Azan Jinnah's taunt that the Congress is a Hindu organization. . . . Let not Bihar, which had done so much to raise the prestige of Congress, be the first to dig its grave." As penance for the Bihar murders, Gandhi announced he would keep himself "on the lowest diet possible," and this would become a "fast unto death if the erring Biharis have not turned over a new leaf." At this juncture, Prime Minister Nehru, Patel, and Liaquat Ali Khan and Abdur Rab Nishtar, two Moslem members of the Nehru cabinet, flew to Bihar. Infuriated by what he saw and heard, Nehru threatened to bomb Bihar from the air if the killings did not cease. "But that was the British way," Gandhi commented.

After a while, Bihar subsided and Calcutta simmered quietly; Gandhi therefore proceeded to Noakhali where frightened Hindus were fleeing before the violence of the Moslem majority.

Noakhali, in the waterlogged delta of the Ganges and Brahmaputra rivers, is one of the least accessible areas of India; some villages can be reached only by rowboat. From Calcutta to Noakhali, both in the same province of Bengal, Phillips Talbot, an American research student, traveled four days by rail, steamer, bicycle, hand-poled ferry and on foot to get to the village where Gandhi was staying. Gandhi would rise at 4 in the morning, walk three or four miles, sometimes in bare feet, to a nearby village, remain there one or two or three days talking and praying incessantly with the inhabitants, and then trek to the next rural settlement. He lived in the huts of peasants who agreed to harbor him, and subsisted on local fruits and vegetables and goat's milk if available. That was his life from November 7, 1946, to March 2, 1947; he had just passed his seventy-seventh birthday. In those four months he lived in 49 villages.

The walking was particularly difficult. He developed chilblains. Often hostile elements strewed filth and brambles on his path between villages. He did not blame them: he said they had been misled by their politicians. In a number of places, the trip from one village to another involved crossing bridges consisting of four or five bamboo poles about four inches in diameter lashed together with jute ropes or vines and supported on bamboo stilts ten or fifteen feet high imbedded in the marshy land. These crude, shaky structures sometimes had one siderail for holding on, sometimes not. Once Gandhi's foot slipped and he might have fallen to the muddy earth far below, but he nimbly regained his balance. To become foot-sure and fearless in such tightrope bridge crossings, he practiced on easier ones a few inches above the ground.

Gandhi deliberately accepted the physical and spiritual challenge presented by this remote region and its 2,500,000 inhabitants, 80 per cent of them Moslem. Month after month, he persevered. "My present mission," he wrote from Noakhali on December 5th, "is the most difficult and complicated one of my life. . . . I am prepared for any eventuality. 'Do or Die' has to be put to the test here. 'Do' here means Hindus and Moslems should learn to live together in peace and amity. Otherwise, I should die in the attempt."

He dispersed his usual retinue; Pyarelal, his sister, Dr. Sushila Nayyar, Sucheta Kripalani, a Bengali, Kanu Gandhi, Kanu's wife, Abha, and others were each sent off to a separate village, often isolated and hostile, and ordered to stay. When Pyarelal was laid low with malaria and dispatched a note to Gandhi asking that his sister be allowed to come and treat him, the Mahatma replied, "If they must fall ill they have to get well or die there. . . . In practice this means that they must be content with home remedies or the therapy of nature's 'five elements.' Dr. Sushila has her own village to look to. . . ." Gandhi subjected himself to the same cruel, unyielding discipline. He had with him only Professor of Anthropology Nirmal Kumar Bose, a former ashramite who served as his Bengali interpreter, Parasuram, his permanent stenographer, to take care of the heavy correspondence, some with Cabinet ministers, which followed him, and Miss Manu Gandhi. The Mahatma helped her prepare the food and clean the hut; he sometimes massaged himself.

At times he must have been desperate. Professor Bose once overheard Gandhi murmuring to himself, "What should I do? What should I do?"

According to the Moslem government of Bengal, 216 persons had been killed in the recent riots in Noakhali and the contiguous Tippera district. Over ten thousand houses had been looted. In Tippera, 9,895 Hindus had been forcibly converted to Islam; in Noakhali the total was greater. Thousands of Hindu women had been abducted and forcibly married to Moslems so that the Hindu community would never take them back. To the same end, Hindus were compelled to slaughter cows and eat meat. Hindu men had to grow beards, twist their loincloths the Moslem instead of the Hindu way, and recite the *Koran*.

At the beginning of Gandhi's Noakhali-Tippera pilgrimage, someone suggested that he urge Hindus to move to other provinces. He passionately rejected such defeatism, because to exchange populations would be an admission of

the impossibility of keeping India united. It would also
deny a basic tenet of Gandhi's faith: that an affinity exists
or can be established between people who think themselves
different. This was now his task. "But I say unto you, Love
your enemies, bless them that curse you, do good to them
that hate you, and pray for them which despitefully use you,
and persecute you. . . . For if ye love them which love
you, what reward have ye?" Thus Jesus spoke. Thus
Gandhi lived and asked others to live. He was once sitting
on a floor of a Moslem hut and discoursing on the beauties
of nonviolence when somebody passed a note to him saying that the man on his right had killed a number of Hindus.
Gandhi smiled faintly and went on speaking. Some time
later several Moslems laid their deadly weapons at his feet.
The poorer Moslems attended his daily prayer meetings in
droves, but wealthy and educated Moslems were threaten-
ing their poor with economic sanctions; Moslem politicians
in Calcutta also discouraged contact with Gandhi. At Nara-
yanpur village, a Moslem gave Gandhi shelter and food.
Gandhi thanked him publicly. Such hospitality was becoming more frequent. Five thousand Hindus and Moslems attended his meeting on January 22nd in Paniala village. He
interrupted services to allow the Moslems to withdraw to
the fringe of the crowd and turn West to Mecca to pray. In
Raipura, one Sunday, Gandhi was guest at a dinner given
by Hindu merchants to two thousand persons, including
caste Hindus, untouchables, Moslems, and Christians; he
felt happy. The Moslem priest took him to the local
mosque. Peasant folk flocked to his hut for comfort and
confession. He told the Hindus not to depend on the military or police, but on their own goodness. "Democracy and
dependence on the military and police are incompatible,"
he taught. In Chandipur village he learned that Hindus who
had fled during the riots were beginning to return. This was
the object of his mission.

Listeners asked him why he had come such a long way;
why had he not reached an agreement with Jinnah instead
of subjecting himself to such a strenuous pilgrimage? A
leader, he replied, is made by his followers. The people
must be at peace among themselves, "then their desire for
neighborly peace would be reflected by their leaders."
Gandhi had gone to Noakhali to create a human bond be-

tween Hindus and Moslems before politics and legal enact-
ments built a wall between them. He was actually in a race
with the politicians. Would his therapy succeed before they
started their surgery?

The scalpels were ready. Late in November, 1946, Prime
Minister Attlee called Nehru, Jinnah, Defense Minister
Baldev Singh, and Liaquat Ali Khan to 10 Downing Street
for an extraordinary conference about the Indian Constituent Assembly scheduled to meet in New Delhi on December 9th. Jinnah had announced that the Moslem League
would not enter the Assembly because Congress rejected
the sectional meetings where Groups A, B, and C would
draft constitutions for the three subfederations. But if the
Moslem League refused to participate in the writing of free
India's constitutions, how could England free India? To
whom would power be transferred? It was to answer these
questions that Attlee summoned the Indian leaders to his
official residence.

During his stay in London, Jinnah declared publicly that
he expected India to be divided into a Hindu state and a
Moslem state, and added that he shared Mr. Churchill's
apprehensions "regarding the possibility of civil war and
riots in India." This statement was read as a warning:
Pakistan or civil war. Inevitably, therefore, the talks at
10 Downing Street ended in disagreement.

On his return to India, Minister Nehru made the long
journey to the village of Srirampur in Noakhali to give
Gandhi a report on the London failure. Gandhi nevertheless insisted that Congress stay out of the sections which
would draw up the constitutions of the three subfederations; he considered them a device to split India. Yet on
January 6, 1947, the All-India Congress Committee, in
defiance of Gandhi, resolved, by a vote of 99 against 52,
to participate in the sections. But this effort to revive the
British Cabinet Mission's plan of May 16, 1946, was late
and futile. The situation had gone beyond that. Prime
Minister Attlee announced in the House of Commons on
February 20th, 1947, that England would quit India "by a
date not later than June, 1948"; Lord (Admiral Louis)
Mountbatten, a great-grandson of Queen Victoria, would
succeed Wavell. He would be the twentieth and last British
Viceroy of India.

Attlee did not say India would be partitioned, but events were now moving very fast. Riots raged in the populous Punjab province, home of Moslems, Sikhs, and Hindus. The Punjab, which was the heart and bulk of the proposed Pakistan's western lobe, and Bengal, its eastern half, had little enthusiasm and gave little support to Pakistan, for being Moslem in their majority they did not fear Hindu domination. Nor did Punjabi and Bengali Moslems feel enough kinship to want to belong together in a national state. Nevertheless, Jinnah's call to direct action swamped reason with passion in both regions, and the Punjab was running with blood. In the first week of March, a resolution of the Congress Working Committee envisaged the "division of the Punjab into two provinces, so that the predominantly Moslem part may be separated from the predominantly non-Moslem part." This was a political watershed. On the one hand, the resolution held up a mirror to the Punjab Moslems and showed them that persistent riots would result in the vivisection of their province. On the other hand, the Congress Working Committee had thereby accepted the principle of a lesser Pakistan, the Pakistan of today.

Disturbed by these developments, and having somewhat calmed Noakhali, Gandhi moved west toward the Punjab. En route, the bloodshed in Bihar stopped him. Without respite, he toured the province. The Bihari Hindus, he stated, "had forgotten in a fit of insanity that they were human beings." He cautioned them against trying to avenge the killing of Hindus by Moslems in the Punjab. That way lay ruin for all India. He urged persons wanted by the police in connection with the riots to surrender to the authorities or to him. Hundreds did. One day a telegram arrived from a Hindu warning the Mahatma not to condemn Hindus for what they had done. He read it to his prayer meeting and replied that "I would forfeit my claim to being a Hindu if I bolstered the wrongdoing of fellow Hindus." He begged Hindus to end their economic boycott of Moslems, but "not one Hindu got up to give the needed assurance. . . . There was small cause for wonder, therefore, if the Moslems were afraid to return to their villages." He told them that if the rioting continued India "might lose the golden apple of independence."

This was the situation on March 22, 1947, when Lord Mountbatten, handsome in white naval uniform, arrived in New Delhi with his wife Edwina, the Vicereine. Their charm and informality immediately won many hearts in circles high and low. Within twenty-four hours, however, Jinnah served notice on Mountbatten that "terrific disasters" awaited India if there was no Pakistan. Four days after his arrival, the new Viceroy invited Jinnah and Gandhi to come to see him. Gandhi was deep in Bihar. Mountbatten offered him a plane. Gandhi preferred the locomotion of the millions. At the Patna station, before the train left, he collected money for Harijan relief. On March 31st, he conferred with Lord Louis for two and a quarter hours. They had five more extended talks between then and April 12th. Jinnah had an equal number of meetings with Mountbatten in the same period. These two weeks and the two months that followed were the most fateful in India's modern history. When the whole dreary process of India's vivisection was over, Mountbatten told his story.

## 29 Round and Round the Mulberry Bush

Lord Mountbatten addressed the Royal Empire Society in London on October 6, 1948, and gave them his side of what happened. In India, he said, Gandhi "was not compared with some great statesman like Roosevelt or Churchill. They classified him simply in their minds with Mohammed and with Christ." In his first encounter with Gandhi, he asked him to tell about his experiences in South Africa. He asked Jinnah about his early life in London. "I just wanted to talk to them to get to know them, to get together and gossip." He told Gandhi and Jinnah separately "a bit about my early life. Then, when I felt I had some sort of understanding with the men I was dealing with, I started talking to them about the problem before us."

Mountbatten's assignment was to take Britain out of India by June, 1948. In order to give the British Parliament time to debate and pass the legislation necessary for this reduction of the Empire, the solution had to be ready by the end of 1947. But on the spot, he and his advisers agreed that this timetable would be too slow; things were happening too quickly. The trouble, Mountbatten explained, had started with Jinnah's Direct Action day on August 16, 1946. There followed the massacre of Hindus in Noakhali and the Hindu reprisals in Bihar, and then the "Moslems massacred the Sikhs at Rawalpindi [in the Punjab]," and an insurrection took place in the Northwest Frontier Province. "I arrived out there," Mountbatten told his audience, "to find this terrible pendulum of massacres swinging wider and wider."

"Personally, I was convinced that the right solution for then and still would have been to keep a United India," under the plan of May 16, 1946, Mountbatten revealed. But this presupposed co-operation between the two parties. "Mr. Jinnah," however, Mountbatten stated, "made it abundantly clear from the first moment that so long as he lived he would never accept a United India. He demanded partition, he insisted on Pakistan. Congress, on the other hand, favored an undivided country, but the Congress leaders agreed that they would accept partition to avoid civil war. Mountbatten "was convinced that the Moslem League would have fought."

But Congress, said Mountbatten, refused to let large non-Moslem areas go to Pakistan. "That automatically meant a partition of the great provinces of the Punjab and Bengal," so that their non-Moslem areas would not be incorporated into Moslem Pakistan. "When I told Mr. Jinnah," Mountbatten confided to the Royal Empire Society, "that I had their [Congress's] provisional agreement to partition he was overjoyed. When I said that it logically followed that this would involve partition of the Punjab and Bengal he was horrified. He produced the strongest arguments why these provinces should not be partitioned. He said they had national characteristics and that partition would be disastrous. I agreed, but I said how much more must I now feel that the same considerations applied to the partitioning of the whole of India. He did not like that, and started explaining why India had to be partitioned, and so we went round and round the mulberry bush until finally he realized that either he could have a United India with an unpartitioned Punjab and Bengal or a divided India with a partitioned Punjab and Bengal, and he finally accepted the latter solution."

So it was decided to bisect India, a country of 400,000,000. Gandhi never agreed. In fact, he hoped to upset the decision.

## 30   The Birth of Two Nations

"Mr. Gandhi," Lord Mountbatten said to the Mahatma in one of their six talks, "today Congress is with me."

"But *India,*" Gandhi replied, "is with me today."

In reporting this exchange to Professor Nirmal Kumar Bose, Gandhi called Mountbatten's boast "cheek," but it was true and it is the key to the partition of India, whereas Gandhi's claim was merely a hope. If India had indeed been with Gandhi he would have reversed the policy of Congress.

Congress ministers had been undergoing a harrowing, traumatic experience inside the Nehru Cabinet, where their Moslem colleagues were using every opportunity and stratagem to hamper the work of the government. Distracted and worn out by daily contact with the undisguised obstructionists in their midst, the Congress Cabinet members and many of their supporters were beginning to fall into the mood of, "Well, if you insist on Pakistan, have it." Nehru put the sentiment into words when he said on April 21, 1947, "The Moslem League can have Pakistan if they wish to have it, but on condition that they do not take other parts of India which do not wish to join Pakistan."

This reluctant acceptance of the lesser Pakistan of today, with Assam, Bengal, and the Punjab divided, was the result of an underestimate of the havoc which partition would produce. In New York on October 16, 1949, Prime Minister Nehru declared that he would have fought to the end against the establishment of Pakistan if he had foreseen the dire consequences which flowed from it. The division of India caused the death of hundreds of thousands of Indians and the uprooting of fifteen million who became refugees. It brought on the war in Kashmir, gigantic economic losses to all parts of the Indian subcontinent, and a continuing religious-nationalistic bitterness with disastrous effects and potentials. Whether or not Gandhi intuitively sensed these dire consequences is irrelevant; he judged and rejected partition not by

its possible results but by its evil essence. This gave him the
energy to fight, whereas the younger leaders were, as an intimate ashram associate of Gandhi put it, "tired and short-
sighted."

The struggle against partition would have delayed independence in the hope of winning freedom for a united country. But numerous Congress leaders, though not of course
its top-rank men, had already smelled the fleshpots of power
and government jobs, and hated to go back to the austerity
of battle. Moreover, the battle might end in prison. Prison
for Gandhi meant relaxation and achievement, for others it
meant suffering. "My stay in prison this time became a
greater ordeal for my nerves than my previous visit had
been," Nehru wrote Gandhi on August 13, 1934. The ordeal
grew progressively worse, and Nehru's last term, from August 9, 1942, to July 14, 1945—almost three years—could
not have made a further period of confinement more en-
ticing, especially since the wisdom of struggle appeared
doubtful to him. Jinnah's threatened civil war had cast its
gory shadow before in the form of recurrent riots; the British
government had no heart, so soon after the Second World
War, to fight the Moslems of India; Mountbatten pictured
partition as inevitable and independence as alluring; he offered the Congress power, Gandhi offered it prison. Against
these formidable facts Gandhi could oppose nothing more
substantial than his undemonstrated assumption that the Indian people were one and that it would be "blasphemy" to
tear them asunder. He knew the weakness of his position;
when he said to Mountbatten, "But *India* is with me today,"
it was really an enunciation of faith and he could not have
expected to be taken at his word. He realized that the burden
of proof was on him.

He therefore left Delhi immediately after his talks with
the Viceroy and returned to Bihar. The province, in April,
was tropically hot, and he could scarcely stand the strain of
extensive travel among the villages. But he did not consider
his body. Peace in Bihar would "dissolve" the trouble in
Calcutta and other parts. His mother, who had no education,
used to tell him, he said, that the atom reflected the universe;
if each person took care of his immediate surroundings the
world would be a better place. General Shah Nawaz, a Moslem whom Gandhi had left in Bihar when he went to Delhi,

reported that Moslems were returning to the villages from which they fled; Gandhi was happy.

At this juncture Nehru telegraphed Gandhi to come to the federal capital; the Congress Working Committee was convening for an historic decision: to approve or not to approve of Pakistan? Gandhi made the five-hundred-mile trip in the suffocating heat of a dusty train.

Nehru favored acceptance as the only escape from an intolerable condition. Vallabhbhai Patel wavered. He would have put Jinnah's civil-war threat to the test of force and meanwhile suppressed the riots with steel. But in the end he too acquiesced. Two and a half years later he explained that he had "agreed to partition as a last resort when we reached a stage when we would have lost all." The alternative seemed to be: Pakistan or a continuation of British rule.

Gandhi made no secret of his chagrin over the Congress decision. "The Congress," he told a prayer meeting in the untouchables' colony in Delhi on May 7th, "has accepted Pakistan and demanded the division of the Punjab and Bengal. I am opposed to any division of India now as I always have been. But what can I do? The only thing I can do is dissociate myself from such a scheme. Nobody can force me to accept it except God." Apparently, God had not intervened.

Gandhi now went to see Mountbatten for a crucial interview. The British, he advised, should quit India with their troops and "take the risk of leaving India to chaos or anarchy." On the surface this looked like nonsense, but it actually hid an astute solution: The British obviously could not abandon India without a government; Gandhi told Mountbatten it should be a Congress government; if England refused, Congress would withdraw from the present provisional Cabinet; then, since the Moslem League minority could not govern India against Congress opposition, Britain, despite her desire to withdraw, would have to remain.

It was impossible, Gandhi felt, for Britain to antagonize the majority in order to placate a minority. Therefore, if Congress did not approve of Pakistan, England would not create it, and if England did not create it there could be no Pakistan.

This strategy, however, would have required the British government, with Congress support, to face up to the menace of Jinnah violence—something it was disinclined to do. Alternatively, in case the British quit India, Congress alone would have had to fight the Moslem League—something it was not inclined to do.

Having grasped these tragic truths, Gandhi rushed across the continent to Calcutta. Pakistan could not be born unless Bengal consented to a surgery that would sever its muscles from its bones, its heart from its brain, its east from its west. "When everything goes wrong at the top," Gandhi asked his Calcutta audience, "can the goodness of the people of the bottom assert itself against the mischievous influence?" This was his desperate dream. Bengal had one language, one culture, one history of resistance to partition by the British early in the century. Would it not rebuff Jinnah now?

After six days of ceaseless work in Calcutta, he traveled to Bihar. Despite the torrid heat, he visited many villages. His refrain was the same: "If the Hindus showed the spirit of brotherliness, it would be good for Bihar, for India, and for the world."

"He is burning the candle at both ends," Sushila Nayyar, his physician, reported. He was striving to stem the tide to partition. If the effort killed him what did it matter? "In the India that is shaping today there is no room for me," he said in a voice quaking with emotion. "I have given up the hope of living 125 years. I may last a year or two."

Meanwhile the British government had made up its mind; it would accept partition if Bengal and the Punjab voted to bisect themselves. "I am of course just as much opposed to the partition of the provinces as I am to the partition of India herself," Mountbattan declared in a New Delhi broadcast. Moreover, his scheme, he said, did not "preclude negotiations between the communities for a united India."

From London, Herbert L. Matthews telegraphed the *New York Times* that "Mr. Gandhi is a very real worry, since if he decides to go on a 'fast unto death' it would well wreck the plan."

On June 15, 1947, the All-India Congress Committee gave the plan its approval by a majority of 153 against 29, with some abstentions. Congress had abandoned Gandhi. Congress President J. B. Kripalani, in an honest speech, explained why. "I," he said, "have seen a well where women and their children, 107 in all, threw themselves to save their honor. In another place, a place of worship, 50 young women were killed by their menfolk for the same reason. . . . These ghastly experiences have no doubt affected my approach to the question. Some members have accused us that we have taken this decision out of fear. I must admit to the charge, but not in the sense in which it is made. The fear is not for the lives lost or the widows' wail or the orphans' cry or the many houses burned. The fear is that if we go on like this, retaliating and heaping indignities on each other, we shall progressively reduce ourselves to a state of cannibalism or worse. . . .

"I have been with Gandhiji for the last thirty years," Kripalani continued. "I joined him in Champaran. I have never swayed in my loyalty to him. . . . Even when I have differed with him I have considered his political instinct to be more correct than my elaborately reasoned attitudes. Today also I feel that he with his supreme fearlessness is correct and my stand is defective." Most of Gandhi's opponents probably felt the same way.

"Why then am I not with him?" Kripalani asked. Why did he not follow Gandhi when he knew Gandhi was right? "It is because," he replied, "he has not yet found a way of tackling the problem on a mass basis." The country was not responding to Gandhi's plea for peace and brotherhood.

This is why Gandhi did not fast. A fast unto death could have prevented Congress from sanctioning partition. What then? It would have broken Congress, which he had nurtured to rule India. He might have done it anyway if the people were with him. "If only non-Moslem India were with me," he affirmed, "I could show the way to undo the proposed partition." But non-Moslem India had deserted him. "I do not agree with what my closest friends have done or are doing," he said.

Thirty-two years of work, Gandhi declared, "have come to an inglorious end." It takes great courage to say that to oneself and in public. It took even greater courage to continue to work in the wreckage of a lifetime's labor. Gandhi now rose to supreme height.

Mahatma Gandhi failed to prevent the partition of India because religious divisions were stronger than nationalistic cohesions. Demagogues appealed more successfully to the feelings that separated Hindus from Moslems than Gandhi, Nehru and others could to the interests that should have united them. The crystals of Indian nationalism were not yet packed together in a hard enough mass to prevent the axe of religion from cutting it in two. Britain granted national freedom to India before India had become a nation; therefore she became two nations. Of these, Pakistan was a religious community struggling to arrive at nationhood, and the Indian Republic a near-nation troubled by provincial isolationism, linguistic differences, and religious hatreds. Gandhi was really the father of a nation still unborn.

Like all human beings, Gandhi must be measured by what he wanted; he wanted one indivisible nation led and peopled by big individuals, free and unafraid in a world similarly constituted. He would not accept less than that. In the last year of his life, therefore, Gandhi must be measured also by what he did not want. His goal had never been the ejection of the British and the substitution of government by Indians. Two-part independence sired by religion out of hate and power lust and delivered in a pool of blood gave him no pleasure. He had the strength and courage to reject it; this is the true dimension of his greatness. India achieved her independence on August 15, 1947, but Gandhi announced that he "cannot participate in the celebrations." He was in Calcutta again fighting riots. Invited to the capital to attend the official inauguration of the nation's life, he refused, and sent no message to the country. All that day he fasted and prayed. "There is disturbance within," he wrote Rajkumari Amrit Kaur the next day. In the midst of festivities his heart was heavy and his mind sad. "Is there something wrong with me," he asked, "or are things really going wrong? I am far away from the condition of equipoise." His *Gita* detachment was impaired. Yet faith never left him. "No cause that is intrinsically just can ever be described as forlorn."

He wrote Rajkumari another letter on August 29th:

"Humanity is an ocean. If a few drops of the ocean are dirty, the ocean does not become dirty." He kept his faith in mankind, and in himself. "I am a born fighter who does not know failure," he assured a Calcutta prayer meeting. Partition was a fact, but "it is always possible by correct conduct to lessen an evil and eventually to bring good out of evil."

He also turned the searchlight inward. "I am groping today," he asserted. He was full of "searching questions." To Kurshed Naoroji he wrote, "I can echo your prayer that I may realize peace and find myself. It is a difficult task but I am after it. O Lord, lead us from darkness into light." He was approaching his seventy-eighth birthday. The world he had built lay partly in ruins about him. Yet he laid plans for the future.

St. Francis of Assisi was hoeing his garden when someone asked what he would do if he were suddenly to learn that he would die before sunset that very day. "I would finish hoeing my garden," he replied. Gandhi continued to hoe his garden.

## 32   Love on Troubled Waters

Gandhi's presence in Calcutta during August, 1947, calmed the interreligious storm, and newspapers paid tributes to the magician in loincloth. But the bisection of Bengal, which was harmful to Moslems and Hindus, again drove them into a mad frenzy. Partition raised more problems than it solved. By the end of the month the sea of hate overflowed into the very home where Gandhi was living. He had just gone to bed on the night of August 31st, when an unruly Hindu mob, carrying the body of a Hindu allegedly stabbed by Moslems, broke into the house with loud yells. They smashed windowpanes with stones and fists, kicked in doors, and tried to tamper with the electric wiring. Gandhi got up to pacify them. "I started shouting at them," he recounted in a letter the next day to Sardar Vallabhbhai Patel, "but who would listen?" Moslems formed a circle to protect him with their bodies. A brick was thrown at him. It struck a Moslem standing by his side. One of the rioters swung a long lathi stick which narrowly missed the Mahatma's head. He shook his head sorrowfully. Finally the police arrived; the police chief appealed to Gandhi to retire to his room. Outside the constables dispersed the crowd with tear gas.

Gandhi decided to fast. In a statement to the press on September 1st, he said, "To put in an appearance before a yelling crowd does not always work. It certainly did not last night. What my word in person cannot do, perhaps my fast will. It may touch the hearts of all the warring factions in the Punjab if it does in Calcutta. I therefore begin fasting from 8:15 tonight to end only if and when sanity returns to Calcutta." It was a fast unto death.

Groups commenced streaming into Gandhi's residence on September 2nd. They would do anything to save his life, they proclaimed. That was the wrong approach, he explained. His fasts were "intended to stir the conscience and remove mental sluggishness." Saving him was secondary to a change of heart. Prominent Moslems came and also an official of the Pakistan Seamen's Union to assure him that they would work for interreligious harmony. On September 4th, the municipality reported that the city had been absolutely peaceful for twenty-four hours. Five hundred policemen, including their British officers, had commenced a one-day sympathy fast while remaining on duty. Burly killers, leaders of hooligan gangs, arrived at Gandhi's bedside and wept at seeing his wasting body; they pledged to refrain from depredations. Hindu, Moslem, and Christian deputations of merchants and workingmen took vows in his presence that there would be no more trouble in Calcutta. He believed them, but this time he wanted it in writing. And before they signed, he said, they must know that if the vow was violated he would commence "an irrevocable fast" which could end only in his death. They withdrew, deliberated, and signed. He thereupon broke his seventy-three hour fast.

From that day, throughout the many months when the Punjab and other provinces shook with religious massacres, Calcutta and the Moslem and Hindu lobes of divided Bengal remained riot-free. Bengal kept its word to the Mahatma.

On September 7th, Gandhi left Calcutta for the Punjab. Another part of his garden needed hoeing. En route, the train stopped at Delhi where Sardar Patel, Health Minister Rajkumari Amrit Kaur, and several associates met him with the gloomy news that riots were raging throughout Delhi.

The Mahatma left the train. His friends told him he would not be safe in the untouchables' quarter which could easily be overrun by thugs. He therefore pitched his camp in the "palatial Birla House," as he called it.

Vital services in New and Old Delhi had been disrupted by the disturbances; no vegetables, milk, or fresh fruits were available. It resembled "a city of the dead." Hindu and Sikh refugees from the Punjab, swarming into Delhi by the thousands and bringing with them authentic as well as exaggerated tales of Moslem atrocities, incited reprisals on Delhi Moslems in which they joined enthusiastically. Murder stalked the streets and nobody was immune.

At Okla, a village fourteen miles from the city, in a region redolent with Moslem tradition and rich in ruins of ancient Mogul forts and mosques, stood Jamia Millia Islamia, a Moslem primary-school-to-college academy, presided over by a friend of Gandhi's, Dr. Zakir Hussain, a stately, bearded scholar with noble head and heart. Ever since August, 1947, the school found itself engulfed in a sea of angry Sikh and Hindu refugees and neighborhood peasants to whom everything Islamic, whether man or edifice, was hateful. At night, the students and teachers stood guard, expecting an assault hourly. In a circle around them they could see Moslem villages in flames and Moslem homes put to the torch. Nearby flows the Jumna. Night after night they could hear howling Moslems jump into the river to escape their pursuers, and then the pursuers would jump in after them, and there were scuffles and splashes and the victim would be held down until he drowned or gave one last anguished screech as the knife descended on his bare throat. Nearer and nearer the ring of violence came to the shivering academy. One dark night, a taxicab arrived at the Jamia Millia grounds; out of it stepped Jawaharlal Nehru. With characteristic physical courage and unconcern he had had himself driven, alone, through the belt of madmen to the threatened Moslem school in order to stay overnight with Dr. Zakir Hussain and give it protection. When Gandhi heard of the academy's danger he went out by car, spent an hour with Dr. Hussain, and addressed the student body. His presence hallowed the spot. After that it remained safe.

On the way back to Birla House, Gandhi visited several refugee camps. He was urged to take an armed guard; Hindus and Sikhs crazed by the deaths and abductions of dear ones might attack him as pro-Moslem. He went without escort. He now developed inordinate energy, undertaking daily inspections of refugee concentrations in the vicinity of the city and touring its riotous wards several times a day. It rained on September 20th. "I think of the poor refugee in Delhi," he told his prayer meeting, "in both East Punjab [in the Indian Republic] and West Punjab [Pakistan] today while it is raining. I have heard that a convoy 57 miles long is pouring into the Indian Union from West Punjab," he said. "It makes my brain reel to think that can be. Such a thing is unparalleled in the history of the world, and it makes me, as it should make you, hang my head in shame."

He was not exaggerating. The 57-mile-long convoy was one of several in the Great Migration in which 15,000,000 unhappy human beings trekked hundreds of miles away from their homes toward distress, disease, and death. Out of the part of the Punjab assigned to Pakistan, moving east in the general direction of Delhi, came millions of Hindus and Sikhs fleeing the knives and clubs of Moslems. Out of the Indian Union, moving toward Pakistan, came millions of Moslems fearing the daggers and lathis of Hindus and Sikhs. A few tired policemen and young volunteers were all that distinguished these convoys from disorganized flights of panicked people. They fled in their bullock carts, or if they had never owned one or it was taken from them, they walked, whole families walked in the dust for weeks, adults carrying children, men carrying the weak and halt in baskets, carrying the aged on their shoulders. Frequently the sick and decrepit were abandoned by the road and left to die. Cholera, smallpox, and similar killers scourged the migrant hordes. Corpses and vultures circling over them marked their route. Sometimes two hostile convoys, advancing in opposite directions, met and, despite flagging energies and myriad cares, continued their senseless vendetta on tilled fields. The Punjab, granary of India, starved, its precious growing grain stamped into the earth by millions of weary feet. The Indian Union felt the pinch of hunger. The Nehru government set up camps outside Delhi to catch the migrants before they could inundate the city. But endless thousands escaped through the cordons, looted shops, slept in doorways, courtyards, gutters, temples, and deserted homes, and disorganized the life of the capital and the government. Reduced to primitive living, the displaced persons yielded to primitive passions which infected those not so situated.

In this city of the mad and the dead, Mahatma Gandhi tried to spread the gospel of love and peace. He planted himself athwart the torrent of boiling passion and spoke with cold reason: molested Moslems must stay; "Hindus and Sikhs who molested them discredited their religion and did irreparable harm to India"; holders of arms should surrender them to him; "driblets have been coming to me voluntarily." He ventured into a meeting of five hundred members of the Rashtriya Sevak Sangha, or R.S.S., a fiercely anti-Moslem, highly-disciplined, para-military body of militant Hindus, and told them they would kill Hinduism by their intolerance; Pakistan atrocities were no justification for Hindu atrocities; "there is no gain in returning evil for evil"; he was indeed a friend of the Moslems, and also of the Hindus and Sikhs; "both sides appear to have gone crazy."

After this speech he invited questions. "Does Hinduism permit killing an evildoer?" an R.S.S. member asked.

"One evildoer cannot punish another," Gandhi replied.

All day he crisscrossed the city, rushing into areas where he heard that blood-thirsty mobs were gathering. The angry human sea parted as he walked among them, face smiling, palms touching in the traditional blessing. The waves of anger subsided. He attended a celebration of 100,000 bearded Sikhs and their families and condemned their violence against Moslems. Sikhs had been drinking and rioting, he charged. "Keep your hearts clean and you will find that all other communities will follow you." At prayer meetings he collected money for blankets for refugees. In refugee camps he told the inmates to spin and to clean their premises. Every evening he asked his prayer congregation, consisting chiefly of Hindus, whether anybody objected to the reading of some verses from the *Koran*. Usually there were two or three objectors. Would the objectors nevertheless remain quiet during the readings? They would. Would the majority resent the objectors? They would not. Then he read the verses. This was a living lesson in tolerance and discipline. Everybody could not agree with everybody else, but they could be nonviolent despite disagreement.

Meanwhile he did not neglect the political future. In the first fortnight of December, 1947, he convened a series of conferences of trusted collaborators outside the government, men and women who had stood by him in his various units for untouchables' welfare, spinning, basic education, nature cure, etcetera, and proposed that they combine into one big society for constructive work and politics, not, however, "to go into politics"—"it would spell ruin"—but "by abjuring power and devoting ourselves to pure selfless service of the voters we can guide and influence them." Unable to steer Congress, he hoped to build a new vehicle which would push the government and, in an emergency, carry the government's load.

"Why could not Congress or the government take over the constructive work?" a delegate asked.

"Because Congressmen aren't sufficiently interested in constructive work," Gandhi replied simply. "We must recognize the fact that the social order of our dreams cannot come through the Congress party of today. . . . There is so much corruption today that it frightens me. Everybody wants to carry so many votes in his pocket because votes give power." Kripalani described the trouble as "red-tapism, jobbery, corruption, bribery, black-marketeering, and profiteering."

Despite Gandhi's unconcealed disappointment with Congress and the government, he was still the key to India's politics, and ministers, from Nehru down, consulted him regularly. He, however, yearned for broader fields of activity. He hoped to go to the Punjab and Pakistan to pacify them. Plans for his trip to Pakistan were already in the making. But he hesitated to leave Delhi. Sporadic violence continued. A Moslem storekeeper, thinking things had settled down, opened the shutters of his shop; a bullet felled him. It was still unsafe for Moslems to be abroad in most sections of the city. Intuitively, Gandhi sensed the possibility of renewed riots. He decided to fast. "It came to me in a flash," he said, and he announced it without consulting Nehru, Patel, or the docto1. This was his last fast and it engraved an image of goodness on India's brain.

## 33 Victory Is to Him Who Is Ready to Pay the Price

Mahatma Gandhi commenced his last fast on the morning of January 13, 1948. He called it an "all-in fast," to death if need be, directed at "the conscience of all," Hindus and Moslems, in both halves of severed India. If everybody responded he would be happy; if one group, say the Sikhs, responded, he would regard it as a miracle and go and live among the Sikhs. He knew he might die, "but death for me would be a glorious deliverance rather than that I should be a helpless witness to the destruction of India, Hinduism, Sikhism, and Islam." His friends must not worry; "I am in God's hands."

The first day he walked to his prayer meeting on the grounds of Birla House and conducted services as usual. Some had taunted him, he said, with fasting for the sake of Moslems. They were right; "All my life I have stood, as everyone should stand, for minorities and those in need. . . . I expect a thorough cleansing of hearts." It did not matter what the Moslems of Pakistan were doing. Hindus and Sikhs should remember Tagore's favorite song: "If No One Responds to Your Call, Walk Alone, Walk Alone."

The second day the doctors told him not to go to prayers, so he dictated a message to be read to the congregation. But when prayer time arrived, he could not resist and went. The fast, he explained, was for the purification of all, himself first. "Supposing there is a wave of self-purification throughout both parts of India!" he exclaimed hopefully. Real amity between the religions would make him "jump like a child," and then his wish to live 125 years would be revived.

He rebuffed his doctors. He did not want to be examined. He refused to drink water with or without salt or citrus juice. His weight dropped two pounds each day. His kidneys were functioning poorly and he was losing strength. He did not care; "I have thrown myself on God."

The third day he submitted to a high colonic irrigation. At 2:30 A.M. he awoke, asked for a hot bath, and in the tub dictated to Pyarelal a statement urging the Nehru government to pay Pakistan 550,000,000 rupees, or approximately $125,000,000, as its share of the assets of the old, united India. Later in the day, Dr. John Matthai, the Finance Minister of the Nehru government, Nehru himself, and Sardar Vallabhbhai Patel visited Gandhi to explain to him why the Cabinet had voted against making the payment. First Dr. Matthai and Nehru stated their reasons, and then Patel spoke for an hour and a half in justification of the refusal. When Patel had finished, Gandhi sat up on his cot, said, "Sardar, you are no longer the Sardar I knew," and burst into tears. Matthai, Nehru, and Patel thereupon withdrew and summoned another Cabinet meeting which, after listening to their report of the Mahatma's reaction, voted to pay the $125,000,000. The sum was paid.

Most of that day an endless queue of Indians and foreigners, thousands upon thousands, passed within ten feet of Gandhi's cot on the enclosed porch of Birla House. He lay, a large part of the time, in a crouched position, like an embryo, with his knees pulled up toward his stomach and his fists under his chest. The body and head were completely covered with a white khadi sheet which framed his face. His eyes were closed and he appeared to be asleep or half conscious. Acute pain was written on the face. Yet somehow, even in sleep or semi-consciousness, the suffering seemed to be sublimated; it was suffering dulled by the exhilaration of faith and moderated by an awareness of service. He seemed fully at peace with himself, and when he awoke he smiled. He tried to go to the prayer meeting but could not stand up so from his bed he spoke into a microphone connected with a loudspeaker at the prayer ground and with the All-India radio which broadcast his words throughout the country. "Do not worry about what others are doing," he began in a weak voice. "Each of us should turn the searchlight inward and purify his or her heart as much as possible. I am convinced that if you purify yourselves sufficiently you will help India and shorten the period of my fast." But they must not think primarily of him. "No one can escape death. Then why be afraid of it? In fact, death is a friend who brings deliverance from suffering." Here he broke down and the rest of his message was read for him. Physicians warned Gandhi the fourth fast day that even if he survived he would suffer serious permanent injury. He had been drinking no water and passing no urine. Unheeding, he spoke to the prayer meeting by microphone for two minutes and boasted that he had "never felt so well on the fourth day of a fast." His voice was stronger too.

January 17, his weight was stabilized at 107 pounds. He sent Pyarelal into the city to ascertain whether it was safe for Moslems to return. Hundreds of telegrams arrived from maharajas, from Moslems in Pakistan, and from all parts of India. He felt gratified but issued a warning that, "Neither the Rajas nor Maharajas nor the Hindus or Sikhs nor any others will serve themselves or India as a whole if at this, what is to me a sacred juncture they mislead me with a view to terminating my fast. They should know that I never feel so happy as when I am fasting for the spirit. This fast has brought me higher happiness than hitherto. No one need disturb this happy state unless he can honestly claim that in his journey he has turned deliberately from Satan toward God." January 18th, he felt better and permitted some light massage. His weight remained at 107 pounds.

Ever since the fast began at 11 A.M. on January 13th, conferences had been meeting in the home of Dr. Rajendra Prasad, the new Congress president, with a view to real peace between divergent elements and not just a cessation of violent attacks. Gandhi had told them that mere paper pledges would not shake his determination to fast till death. He asked pledges plus detailed plans for their implementation. The delegates must not promise more than they knew their followers were ready to carry out. For five days they had been talking, debating, drafting, consulting colleagues, consulting consciences. Finally, on the morning of January 18th, one hundred Hindu, Sikh, Moslem, Christian, and Jewish conferees, plus representatives of the militant R.S.S. and Hindu Mahasabha, plus the High Commissioner of Pakistan, and Prasad, Nehru, and Azad, presented themselves before Gandhi. They undertook, in writing, to "protect the life, property, and faith" of Moslems, and guaranteed free circulation of Moslems in areas where they had feared to appear. Mosques would be returned and their Hindu refugee occupants evacuated, and Mohammedan businessmen who had fled or were in hiding could resume their activity. All these improvements would be introduced without benefit of police or military; the people would see to them. As earnest of the change, touching scenes of Hindu-Moslem fraternization had already taken place and they were described to the fasting, tired Mahatma.

He now raised himself on his cot, feeble yet vibrant, and addressed the delegates. The press had reported atrocities in Allahabad, he said. He plainly indicated that the R.S.S. and Hindu Mahasabha, whose officials were in the room, bore the responsibility. "If you cannot make the whole of India realize that the Hindus, Sikhs, and Moslems are all brothers," he declared, "it will bode ill for both Dominions. What will happen to India if they both quarrel?" This thought shook him and tears rolled down his hollow cheeks. Onlookers sobbed. When he regained control his voice was too weak to be heard and he whispered his remarks into the ear of Dr. Sushila Nayyar who repeated them aloud. Were they deceiving him? Were they trying to save his life? He wanted to go to Pakistan. Would they release him by keeping the peace? Maulana Azad, the Congress Moslem leader, R.S.S. spokesmen, the Pakistan ambassador, and a Sikh made reassuring, pleading statements. Gandhi sat on his cot, silent and sunk in thought. At that moment he was deciding whether he should die. He announced he would break the fast. First Parsi, Moslem, and Japanese scriptures were read and then the Hindu verse:

> Lead me from untruth to truth,
> From darkness to light,
> From death to immortality.

Then girls of the ashram sang a Hindu hymn and "When I Survey the Wondrous Cross," Gandhi's favorite Christian hymn. At last, the Mahatma accepted a glass filled with eight ounces of orange juice and slowly drank it. He interrupted to say that if the peace pledges were kept it would revive his wish to live 125 years, or maybe even 133. The same afternoon, he had a talk with Arthur Moore, former editor of the British-owned daily *Statesman* who reported that Gandhi "was lightsome and gay, and his interest while he talked with me was not in himself but in me, whom he plied with probing questions."

Addressing the prayer meeting that evening, Gandhi interpreted the pledges as meaning, "Come what may, there will be complete friendship between the Hindus, Moslems, Sikhs, Christians, and Jews, a friendship not to be broken." That this was more than the pious delusion of a man seeking balm was the testimony of Sir Mohamed Zafrullah Khan, Pakistan Foreign Minister, who told the United Nations Security Council at Lake Success, "A new and tremendous wave of feeling and desire for friendship between the two Dominions is sweeping the subcontinent in response to the fast." Verily a magician. If only politicians had not interfered. The end of the fast restored his habitual gaiety, and he returned to work with vigor. He found a new lease on life because he had fearlessly faced death.

## 34 Death Before Prayers

The first day after his fast Gandhi was carried to prayers in a chair. In his speech, only faintly audible through the microphone, he reported that an official of the Hindu Mahasabha, which believed in Hindu supremacy and was the ideological parent of the militant R.S.S., had repudiated the Delhi peace pledge. Gandhi expressed his regret.

While the Mahatma was addressing the prayer meeting the next evening the noise of an explosion was heard. The audience became agitated. "Don't worry about it," Gandhi urged. "Listen to me." A handmade bomb had been thrown at him from the nearby garden wall.

The following day Gandhi walked to the prayer ground—the first time since the fast. Congratulations had poured in on him, he reported, for remaining unruffled during the bombing incident. He made light of it. "I would deserve praise," he said, "only if I fell as a result of such an explosion and yet retained a smile on my face and no malice for the doer. No one should look down on the misguided youth who had thrown the bomb. He probably looks upon me as an enemy of Hinduism." He begged the young man to remember that "those who differ with him are not necessarily evil" and he asked the congregation to pity the "miscreant" and try to convert him.

The young man was Madan Lal, refugee from the Punjab who lived in a Delhi mosque until the police, in accordance with the peace pledge made to Gandhi, commenced clearing Moslem places of worship. "I had seen with my own eyes horrible things in Pakistan," he testified at his trial. "I had also been an eyewitness to the shooting down of Hindus in the Punjab towns. . . ." Infuriated, he joined an R.S.S. conspiracy to kill Gandhi. When he was arrested after his hand grenade had failed to attain Gandhi, Nathuram Vinayak Godse, a fellow conspirator, came up to Delhi from Bombay. Godse, aged thirty-five, was the editor and publisher of a Hindu Mahasabha weekly in Poona, and a high-degree Brahman. He and Madan Lal and seven other plotters were tried together; the trial lasted more than six months. "I sat brooding intensely on the atrocities perpetrated on Hinduism and its dark and deadly future if left to face Islam outside and Gandhi inside," Godse affirmed on the witness stand, "and . . . I decided all of a sudden to take the extreme step against Gandhi." The success of Gandhi's recent fast especially incensed Godse and Madan Lal. They were baffled by the Mahatma's authority and found no weapon against it. Lal, in his evidence, stated that he was exasperated by the payment of the 550,000,000 rupees to Pakistan.

After Lal's arrest—an illiterate old woman had grappled with him and held him till the police arrived—Godse began loitering around Birla House. In the pocket of his khaki jacket he concealed a small pistol.

Sunday, January 25, 1948, the prayer meeting attendance was especially heavy. Pleased, Gandhi told the worshippers to bring straw mats or thick khadi to sit on because the ground in winter was cold and damp. It gladdened his heart, he said, to learn that Hindus and Moslems were experiencing "a reunion of hearts," Would each Hindu and each Sikh who came to prayers hereafter bring along "at least one Moslem" as a concrete manifestation of brotherhood? Godse, lurking in the multitude, could not have agreed. Why, he and his co-conspirators argued, should Moslems go to Hindu prayers? Why should the *Koran* be read by a Hindu mahatma? If they could only get rid of Gandhi the Moslems would be defenseless and then the Hindus would be free to attack Pakistan and reunite India.

Godse raged, but bided his time. Government ministers pressed Gandhi to accept a guard and have worshippers searched. The idea repelled him.

Prime Minister Nehru and Deputy Prime Minister Sardar Patel did not see eye to eye on many issues. They were temperamental opposites. The friction between them worried Gandhi. He wondered whether they could stay together in the same Cabinet. It seemed that he might have to make a choice and ask the other to resign. They had put the situation in his lap. He loved Nehru and felt sure of his impartial friendship for Hindus, Sikhs, and Moslems. Patel, however, was a statesman and a skilled administrator; his departure would have crippled the government. Finally, Gandhi decided against sacrificing either; they were indispensable to one another. The Mahatma accordingly wrote a note in English to Nehru saying they "must hold together." At 4 P.M. on January 30th, Patel came to hear the same message from Gandhi's lips. At 4:30, Gandhi's last supper was brought in, consisting of goat's milk, cooked and raw vegetables, oranges, and a concoction of ginger, sour lemons, and strained butter with juice of aloe. As he ate they talked. It was now five o'clock, and Abha, knowing Gandhi's devotion to punctuality, held up his nickel-plated watch. "I must tear myself away," he said to Patel and walked quickly to the prayer ground. Five hundred men and women were waiting for him. "I am late by ten minutes," he remarked to Abha and Manu, on whose shoulders he was leaning. "I hate being late. I should have been here on the stroke of five." So saying, he quickly cleared the five steps up to the level of the prayer ground. He was now only a few yards from the wooden platform on which he sat during services. Most of the people rose; many edged forward to be closer to him; those nearest to him bowed to his feet. Gandhi lifted his arms, smiled, and touched his palms together in the traditional greeting-blessing.

Godse had moved into the front row, his hand on the pistol in his pocket. He had no personal hatred of Gandhi, Godse stated at his trial at which he was sentenced to be hanged: "Before I fired the shots I actually wished him well and bowed to him in reverence." He stood in the path of the Mahatma and bowed. Manu tried to brush him aside so Gandhi could start services without further delay. Godse pushed her away, and, planting himself two feet in front of the Mahatma, fired three times. The smile faded from Gandhi's face and his arms descended to his sides. "Oh, God," he murmured, and was instantly dead.

His legacy is courage, his lesson truth, his weapon love.
His life is his monument.
He now belongs to mankind.

# INDEX